Bible St
Young

CRACE
Being Loved, Loving God

Clifton F. Guthrie

Abingdon Press

Nashville

Grace: Being Loved, Loving God
20/30: Bible Study for Young Adults

by Clifton F. Guthrie

ISBN 0-687-02821-3
ISBN 978-0-687-02821-4

This book is printed on acid-free paper.

MANUFACTURED IN THE UNITED STATES OF AMERICA.

07 08 09 10 11—10 9 8 7 6 5 4 3

CONTENTS

ΜEET THE WRITER

CLIFTON F. GUTHRIE is Assistant Professor of Homiletics and Pastoral Studies at Bangor Theological Seminary in Bangor, Maine. He currently serves as the co-editor of *Doxology: A Journal of Worship.*

Cliff has extensive teaching background at Candler School of Theology as well, having taught courses on systematic theology, preaching, United Methodist history, and worship and spirituality. His writing and editing credits include *For all the Saints: A Calendar of Commemorations for United Methodists* and numerous reviews and articles on the Christian calendar, pastoral care and practice, and worship issues. Cliff has offered papers and presentations at various academic society events.

Cliff has previously served as a local church pastor and youth minister and as an editor at The United Methodist Publishing House. He and his family reside in Bangor, Maine.

WELCOME TO 20/30:
BIBLE STUDY
FOR YOUNG ADULTS

The *20/30* Bible study series is offered for post-modern adults who want to participate in and help structure their own discoveries—in life, in relationships, in faith. In each of the volumes of this series, we will have the opportunity to use our own experience in life and faith to examine the biblical texts in new ways. We will examine biblical images that shape all of our lives, even if we are not immediately aware that they do.

Image Is Everything

Images are what shape our decisions. We may think or know certain important data that weigh heavily in a decision. We may value the advice and counsel of others. We may find that the stated or implied wishes of others influence what we do. But in the end, it is often the *image* we hold that makes the decision.

For example, perhaps you were deeply hurt by someone important to you—an employer, a friend, even a pastor. You know in your heart that the institution is not to blame or that friendships are based on more than one event. But the image shaped by the difficult experience is that the job, or the friend, or the church cannot be relied upon. You *know* better, but you just have to make a change anyway. The image was more powerful than the reason.

Images are powerful, and they are familiar. In each of the studies in this series, you will encounter a well-known image that will connect your familiar experiences with scriptural content.

Have you ever felt that you wanted to get closer to God but didn't deserve to even try? *Grace: Being Loved, Loving God* explores God's love for us and how "it isn't something we earn but something that is"; how that love leads us into relationship with God and with others; and how our hearts and lives are changed as we use the gifts God has given us to build community, growing toward perfect love.

You juggle multiple demands—school or work, family, friends, church, day-to-day "stuff" like paying bills and dealing with junk mail—but do these activities each receive the proper priority at the proper time? *Balance: Living With Life's Demands* helps you sort through various claims on your life and put your priorities into a healthy and manageable perspective.

You define for yourself what you think is "the good life." Is your definition complete? *Abundance: Living Responsibly With God's Gifts* provides a guide into the biblical understanding of abundant life and sorts out many of the faithful and practical issues that come together in a life of abundance.

When you love and you are loved in return, you know that love is more than just a matter of emotion. *Love: Opening Your Heart to God and Others* is a guide into biblical understandings of love and explores many facets of love, and love gone wrong, with God, family, friends, and life partner.

You have faith, but you also realize that it can mean many things. Is it belief or trust, or waiting, or moral behavior, or something else? Or is it all those things? *Faith: Living a Spirited Life* examines your faith and growth as Christians.

You know what it is like to make agreements, to establish commitments, to give your word and expect to be trusted. *Covenant: Making Commitments That Count* study sessions explain a variety of covenants, what happens when covenants are broken, how to have a faithful covenant to care for others and for the earth; and certainly, what it means to have this sacred covenant with God.

You know what it is like to move to a new place, to have to deal with transitions in school or work or in relationships. You have probably experienced changes in your family as you have grown up and moved out on your own. Some of these moves are gradual, just taken in stride. Others can be painful or abrupt; certainly life-changing. In *Exodus: Leaving Behind, Moving On,* you learn how God is in the midst of those movements, no matter how minor or how transformational.

You know how important it is to have a sense of support and roots: to have friends and a life partner. *Community: Living Faithfully With Others* examines Scriptures and life examples that delve into intimacy, work and family relationships, and more.

Experience, Faith, Growth, and Action

Each volume in this series will help you probe, on your own terms, how your experience links with your faith and how deepening your faith develops your life experience. As a prompt for reflection, each volume has several pages of real-life case studies. To foster growth in faith and commitment to Jesus Christ, ways to be involved in specific service opportunities are listed on pages 79-80.

We hope this series will support encountering God through Scripture, reflection, and dialogue in a community of faith devoted to growth in faith and seeing others grow in faith, and to serve others. One image we hold is that God is in all things. God is certainly with you.

HOW TO USE THIS RESOURCE

Each session of this resource includes similar components or elements:

- A statement of the issue or question to be explored
- Several "voices" of persons who are currently dealing with that issue
- Exploration of biblical passages relating to the question raised
- "Biblical Studies 101" boxes that provide insight about the study of the Bible
- Questions for reflection and discussion
- Suggested individual and group activities designed to bring the session to life
- Optional case studies (found in the back of the book)
- Various service learning activities related to the session (found in the back of the book)

Choices, Choices, Choices

Collectively, these components mean one thing: *choice*. You have choices to make concerning how to use each session of this resource. Want just the nitty-gritty Bible reading, reflection, and study for personal or group use? Then focus your attention on just those components during your study time.

Like starting with real-life stories about issues then moving into how the Bible might be relevant? Start with the "voices" and move on from there. Use the "voices" to encourage group members to speak about their own experiences.

Prefer highly charged discussion encounters where many different viewpoints can be heard? Start the session with the biblical passages, followed by the questions and group activities. Be sure to compare the ideas found in the "Biblical Studies 101" boxes with your current ideas for more discussion. Want the major challenge of applying biblical principles to a difficult problem? After reading the biblical material, read one of the case studies, using the guidelines provided on page 14, or get involved with one of the service learning options described on pages 79-80.

Great Versatility

This resource has been designed for many different uses. Some persons will use this resource for personal study and reflection. Others will want to explore the work with a small group of friends. And still others will see this book as a different type of Sunday school resource.

Spend some time thinking about your own questions. study habits, and learning styles or those of your small group. Then use the guidelines mentioned above to fashion each session into a unique Bible study session to meet those requirements.

Highly Participatory

As you will see, the Scriptures. "voices." commentary. and experience of group members will provide an opportunity for an active, engaging time together. The greatest challenge for a group leader might be "crowd control" —being sure everyone has the chance to put his or her ideas into the mix!

The Scriptures will help you and those who study with you to make connections between real-life issues and the Bible. This resource values and encourages personal participation as a means to understand fully and appreciate the intersection of personal belief with God's ongoing work in each and every life.

ON ORGANIZING A SMALL GROUP

Learning with a small group of persons offers certain advantages over studying by yourself. First, you will hopefully encounter different opinions and ideas, making the experience of Bible study a richer and more challenging event. Second, any leadership responsibilities can be shared among group members. Third, different persons will bring different talents. Some will be deep thinkers while other group members will be creative giants. Some persons will be newcomers to the Bible; their questions and comments will help others clarify their deeply held assumptions.

So how does one go about forming a small group? Follow the steps below and see how easy this task can be.

- **Read through the resource carefully.** Think about the ideas presented, the questions raised, and the exercises suggested. If the sessions of this work excite you, it will be easier for you to spread your enthusiasm to others.

- **Spend some time thinking about church members, friends, and coworkers who might find the sessions of this resource interesting**. On a sheet of paper, list two characteristics or talents you see in each person that would make him or her an attractive Bible study group member. Some talents might include "deep thinker," "creative wizard," or "committed Christian." Remember: The best small group has members who differ in learning styles, talents, ideas, and convictions, but who respect the dignity and integrity of the other members.

- **Most functional small groups have seven to fifteen members.** Make a list of potential group members that doubles your target number. For instance, if you would like a small group of seven to ten members, be prepared to invite fourteen to twenty persons.

- **Once your list of potential candidates is complete, decide on a tentative location and time.** Of course, the details can be negotiated with those persons who accept the invitation, but you need to sound definitive and clear to perspective group members. "We will initially set Wednesday night from 7 to 9 p.m. at my house for our meeting time" will sound more attractive than "Well, I don't know either when or where we would be meeting, but I hope you will consider joining us."

- **Make initial contact with prospective group members short, sweet, and to the point.** Say something like. "We are putting together a Bible study using a different kind of resource. When would be a good time to show you the resource and talk about the study?" Establishing a special time to make the invitation takes the pressure off the prospective group member to make a quick decision.

- **Show up at the decided time and place.** Talk with each prospective member individually. Bring a copy of the resource with you. Show each person what excites you about the study and mention the two unique characteristics or talents you feel he or she would offer the group. Tell each person the initial meeting time and location and how many weeks the small group will meet. Also mention that the need for a new time or location could be discussed during the first group meeting. Ask for a commitment to come to the first session. Thank individuals for their time.

- **Give a quick phone call or e-mail to thank all persons for their consideration and interest.** Remind persons of the time and location of the first meeting.

- **Be organized.** Use the first group meeting to get acquainted. Briefly describe the seven sessions. Have a book for each group member, and discuss sharing responsibilities for leadership.

LEADING AND SHARING LEADERSHIP

So the responsibility to lead the group has fallen upon you? Don't sweat it. Follow these simple suggestions and you will razzle and dazzle the group with your expertise.

■ **Read the session carefully.** Look up all the Bible passages. Take careful notes about the ideas, statements, questions, and activities in the session. Try all the activities.

■ **Using twenty to twenty-five blank index cards, write one idea, activity, Bible passage, or question from the session on each card** until you either run out of material or cards. Be sure to look at the case studies and service learning options.

■ **Spend a few moments thinking about the members of your group.** How many like to think about ideas, concepts, or problems? How many need to "feel into" an idea by storytelling, worship, prayer, or group activities? Who are the "actors" who prefer a hands-on or participatory approach, such as an art project or simulation, to grasp an idea? List the names of all group members, and record whether you believe each to be a THINKER, FEELER, or ACTOR.

■ **Place all the index cards in front of you in the order in which they originally appeared in the session.** Looking at that order, ask yourself: 1) Where is the "Head" of the session—the key ideas or concepts? 2) Where is the "Heart" of the session in which persons will have a deep feeling response? 3) Where are the "feet"—those activities that ask the group to put the ideas and feelings to use? Separate the cards into three stacks: HEAD, HEART, and FEET.

■ **Now construct the "body" for your class.** Shift the cards around, using a balance of HEAD, HEART, and FEET cards to determine which activities you will do and in what order. This will be your group's unique lesson plan. Try to choose as many cards as you have group members. Then, match the cards: HEAD and THINKERS; HEART and FEELERS; FEET and ACTORS for each member of the group. Don't forget a card for yourself. If your group has ten members, you should have about ten cards.

■ **Develop the leadership plan.** Invite these group members prior to the session to assist in the leadership. Show them the unique lesson plan you developed. Ask for their assistance in developing and/or leading each segment of the session as well as an ice-breaking introduction and a closing ritual or worship experience.

Your lesson plan should start with welcoming the participants. Hopefully everyone will have read the session ahead of time. Then, begin to move through the activity cards in the order of your unique session plan, sharing the leadership as you have agreed.

You may have chosen to have all the HEAD activities together, followed by the HEART cards. This would introduce the session's content, followed by helping group members "feel into" the issue through interactive stories, questions, and exercises with all group members. Feel free to add more storytelling, discussion, prayer, meditation, or worship.

You may next have chosen to use the FEET cards to end the session. Ask the group, "What difference should this session make in our daily lives?" You or the ACTORS should introduce the FEET cards as possible ways to discern a response. Ensuring that group members leave with a few practical suggestions for doing something different during the week is the point of this section of the unique lesson plan.

■ **Remember: Leading the group does not mean "Do it all yourself."** With a little planning, you can enlist the talents of many group members. By inviting group members to lead parts of the session that feel comfortable for them, you will model and encourage shared leadership. Welcome their interests in music, prayer, worship, Bible, and so on, to develop innovative and creative Bible study sessions that can transform lives in the name of Jesus Christ.

CHOOSING TEACHING OPTIONS

This young adult series was designed, written, and produced out of an understanding of the attributes, concerns, joys, and faith issues of young adults. With great care and integrity, this image-based print resource was developed to connect biblical events and relationships with contemporary, real-life situations of young adults. Its pages will promote Christian relationships and community, support new biblical learning, encourage spiritual development, and empower faithful decision-making and action.

This study is well-suited to young adults and may be used confidently and effectively. But with the great diversity within the young adult population, not every line of this study will be written "just for you." To be most relevant, some portions of the study material need to be tailored to fit your particular group. Adjustments for a good fit involve making choices from options offered by the resource. This customizing may be done easily by a designated leader who is familiar with the layout of the resource and the young adults who are using it.

What to Expect

In this study Scripture and real-life images mesh together to provoke a personal response. Young adults will find themselves thinking, feeling, imagining, questioning, making decisions, professing faith, building connections, inviting discipleship, taking action, and making a difference. Scripture is at the core of each session. Scenarios weave in the dimensions of real life. Narrative and text boxes frame plenty of teaching options to offer young adults.

Each session is part of a cohesive volume, but it is designed to stand alone. One session is not dependent on knowledge or experience accumulated from other sessions. A group leader can freely choose from the teaching options in an individual session without wondering about how it might affect the other sessions.

A Good Fit

For a better fit, alter the session based on what is known about the young adult participants. Young adults are a diverse constituency with varied experiences, interests, needs, and values. There is really no single defining characteristic that links young adults. Specific information about the age, employment status. household. personal relationships. and lifestyle among participants will equip a leader to make choices that ensure a good fit.

■ **Customize.** Read through the session. Notice how scenarios and teaching options move from integrating Scripture and real-life dimensions to inviting a response.

■ **Look at the scenario(s).** How real is the presentation of real life? Say that the main character is a professional. white male. married, in his early twenties, and caught in a workplace dilemma that entangles his immediate superior and a subordinate from his division. Perhaps your group members are mostly college students and recent graduates. unmarried. and still on the way to being "settled." There are many differences between the man in the scenario and these group members.

As a leader, you could choose to eliminate the case study. substitute it with another scenario (there are several more choices on pages 76-78), claim the validity of the dilemma and shift the spotlight from the main character to the subordinate. or modify the description of the main character. Break-out groups based on age or employment experience might also be used to accommodate the differences and offer a better fit.

■ **Look at the teaching options.** How are the activities propelling participants toward a personal response? Perhaps the Scripture study requires more meditative quiet than is possible and a more academic, verbal, or artistic approach would offer a better fit. Maybe more direct decisions or actions would fit better than more passive or logical means. Try to keep a balance, though, that allows participants to "get out of their head" to reflect and also to move toward action.

Conceivably, there could just be too much in any one session. As a leader, you can pick and choose among teaching options, substitute case studies, take two meetings to do one session. and adapt any process to make a better fit. The tailoring process can be evaluated as adjustments are made. Judge the fit every time you meet. Ask questions that gauge relevance, and assess how the resource has stretched minds. encouraged discipleship, and changed lives.

USING BREAK-OUT GROUPS

20/30 break-out groups are small groups that encourage the personal sharing of lives and the gospel. The word *break-out* is a sweeping term that includes a variety of small group settings. A break-out group may resemble a Bible study group, an interest group, a sharing group, or other types of Christian fellowship groups.

Break-out groups offer young adults a chance to belong and personally relate to one another. Members are known, nurtured, and heard by others. Young adults may agree and disagree while maximizing the exchange of ideas, information, or options. They might explore, confront, and resolve personal issues and feelings with empathy and support. Participants can challenge and hold each other accountable to a personalized faith and stretch its links to real life and service.

Forming Break-out Groups

The nature of these small break-out groups will depend on the context and design of the specific session. On occasion the total group of participants will be divided for a particular activity. Break-out groups will differ from one session to the next. Variations may involve the size of the group, how group members are divided, or the task of the group. Break-out groups may also be used to accommodate differences and help tailor the session plan for a better fit. In some sessions, specific group assembly instructions will be provided. For other sessions, decisions regarding the size or division of small groups will be made by the designated leader. Break-out groups may be in the form of pairs or trios, family-sized groups of three to six members, or groups of up to ten members.

They may be arranged simply by grouping persons seated next to one another or in more intentional ways by common interests, characteristics, or life experience. Consider creating break-out groups according to age; gender; type of household, living arrangements, or love relationships; vocation, occupation, career, or employment status; common or built-in connections; lifestyle; values or perspective; or personal interests or traits.

Membership

The membership of break-out groups will vary from session to session, or even within specific sessions. Young adults need to work at knowing and being known, so that there can be a balance between break-out groups that are more similar and those that reflect greater diversity. There may be times when more honest communication, trust, or accountability may be desired and group leaders will need to be free to self-select members for small groups.

It is important for *20/30* break-out groups to practice acceptance and to value the worth of others. The potential for small groups to encourage personal sharing and significant relationships is enhanced when members agree to exercise active listening skills, keep confidences, expect authenticity, foster trust, and develop ways of loving one another. All group members contribute to the development and function of break-out groups. Designated leaders especially need to model manners of hospitality and help ensure that each group member is respected.

Invitational Listening

Consider establishing an "invitational listening" routine that validates the perspective and affirms the voice of each group member. After a question or statement is posed, pause and allow time to think—not all persons think on their feet or talk out loud to think. Then, initiate conversation by inviting one group member, by name, to talk. This person may either choose to talk or to "pass." Either way, this person is honored and is offered an opportunity to speak and be heard. This person carries on the ritual by inviting another group member, by name, to speak. The process continues until all have been invited, by name, to talk. As each one invites another, the responsibility of acceptance and hospitality in the break-out groups is shared among all its members.

Study group members break-out to belong, to share the gospel, to care, and to watch over one another in Christian love. "So deeply do we care for you that we are determined to share with you not only the gospel of God but also our own selves, because you have become very dear to us" (1 Thessalonians 2:8).

GRACE:
BEING LOVED, LOVING GOD

Grace is a notion that is hard for many of us to grasp. We live in a crazy, schizophrenic culture. On the one hand, the American myth admonishes us that ours is a land of opportunity and that all that stands between us and success or riches is hard work. On the other hand, if that theory does not work out for you (that is, you are not lazy, but you are not rich either), you can always lose yourself to a life of fantasy or addiction. Those of us who work hard but never see the riches flow in are compensated by entertainment. Game shows and lotteries fascinate us. A flood of Hollywood images wash over us featuring an ordinary person who, after a mystical lightening strike, a visit from an alien or angel, or laboratory accident (pick one), suddenly finds wealth, skill, adventure, a perfect body, or a perfect love without having to spend the lifetime of hard work we secretly know they require in real life. In American pop mythology (which we are exporting now through the world), the good life comes to us either because we pull ourselves up by the bootstraps or because we are lucky. Otherwise we are sunk.

From Fantasy to Grace

Judging from the stories we in which we swim, it is much easier for us to engage in fantasy than it is to live in grace. That there might be a power of acceptance shot through the universe; a scarlet thread running through everything there is and ever will be; a love that covers us like an old quilt; a God that gives not one whit about what we own, how much we weigh, how we dress, or who we love—what an odd thing on which to stake one's life.

But there's the rub. The basic Christian message is that God's self is communicated to the whole of creation and to humanity freely, with unmerited, forgiving, absolute love, and asks us to trust that love. Love isn't something we earn, but something that is. God does not grant us grace because we are unique or special. We aren't. We share 98.4 percent of our DNA with common and pygmy chimpanzees. Scientifically speaking, we are essentially just another primate, the "Third Chimpanzee," as Jared Diamond, a professor of physiology, has said. Christians have too often asserted that humans are immeasureably different from the earth and its creatures, and so we live alienated from our own planet, poisoning it and ourselves as we dubiously remake it in our own image.

Genesis affirms, however, that human beings have been made *from* the earth, yet *in* the image and likeness of God (Genesis 1:26). We emerge from the story of Creation as all other creatures; but we are made in God's image, too.

Imago Dei: The God Within

In Western theology there has long been a attempt to pinpoint exactly where that *imago Dei* (the image of God) can be found in us: Is it in our intellect? our will? the soul? our capacity for language? Notice that all of these focus on qualities that make us different from other animals. But Easter theology kept a strong tradition of seeing that what sustains humanity as the image of God is not a quality in *us*, but a quality in *God*. God has chosen to be in relationship with us, and has proven that time and again. This is something that we cannot shake, deny it as much as we want. God is the "Hound of Heaven at My Heels," as the poem by Francis Thompson said it.

God keeps pursuing us with grace to have a deeper, more honest, and more daring relationship with God and with others. Grace is not given that we may feel better about ourselves but that we may ourselves be better. *Grace* is the religious word for the many ways that God woos. pressures, supports, invites, charms, moves, beguiles, nudges, calls, scares. prods, pokes, and persuades us to love.

But nothing about grace is coercive. Nothing removes our capacity to say no to this reality or to choose to ignore it. We are free to pursue our self-interest. We may respond or not respond to these pleas to become more intimately acquainted with the holy mystery. Those who do respond sense themselves on an exciting journey as that grace reaches down to the very depths of one's shame, sorrow, fear, distrust, and selfishness and emancipates them for the sake of love.

But this is one adventure that is hard work not fantasy. Visits from angels and aliens are highly unlikely. And it is improbable that wealth, success, and good looks will come your way, although your friends may comment that something has come over you, though they cannot quite put their finger on it. Grace. The ultimate gift.

BEING GRACEFUL

> This session is designed to examine three typical ways in which the word *grace* is used.

GRACE LIVES WHERE?

A magazine advertisement calls attention to a new sport-utility vehicle by parking it in front of Frank Lloyd Wright's Guggenheim Museum of Art in New York City. "Grace lives here," the ad gushes.

Since we live in an age when an SUV can become an icon of grace, it may be wise for anyone studying the meaning of grace in the Bible to spend some time considering the word.

There are three basic meanings for the noun *grace*, and all three can be found in the Bible. The last two we will consider in this session get much more attention than the first for reasons we will soon discover.

START Introduce yourselves to one another, or check in with one another if your group is already well acquainted.

Grace Lives Where?

LOOK CLOSER

As an opening exercise, try expressing your understanding of the concept of grace without using any words. Be creative. Use your hands to form a sculpture, draw a simple picture, or use some objects you find around the room. Keep these gestures in mind as there will be an opportunity at the end of the session to return to them.

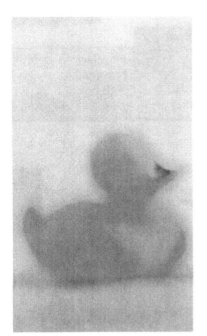

GRACE IS CHARMING

Grace can mean "elegance," "refined beauty," or "charm." Something is "graceful" if it has a pleasing quality. For instance, we might describe the moves of a dancer or the lines of a building (or an SUV, apparently) as graceful. Consider these classic uses of the word:

"Grace was in all her steps, heaven in her eyes. In every gesture dignity and love" (Adam describing Eve in John Milton's *Paradise Lost*, Book VIII, line 488).

"Youth, large, lusty, loving—Youth, full of grace, force fascination! Do you know that Old Age may come after you, with equal grace, force, fascination?" (Walt Whitman, *Youth, Day; Old Age and Night*).

"Get place and wealth, if possible, with grace; If not, by any means get wealth and place" (Alexander Pope [1688–1744] from *Satires, Epistles, and Odes of Horace,* Epistle 1, Book 1, line 103).

In the Hellenistic (Greek) culture that surrounded the ancient Mediterranean world of Jesus' day, this use of *grace* (Greek *charis*) to mean "beauty" or "elegance" was common. In fact, in Greek and Roman mythology, the "Graces" (Greek *Charites*) were three sister goddesses named Aglaia, Euphrosyne, and Thalia who dispensed charm and beauty.

This meaning of *grace* or *gracious* can be found in the Bible too but sometimes with a twist.

Read Luke 4:16-30. Discuss: What might Jesus have been feeling as he came back to his hometown synagogue? Do you think Jesus' actions in this story are appropriate? Why or why not? Have you ever felt like you wanted to go back to an old church or school and "tell them off"? What about?

FROM MAN OF THE YEAR TO ATTEMPTED MANSLAUGHTER (OR THE UNGRACEFUL JESUS)

Read Luke 4:16-30.

After being tempted in the desert and launched into a teaching ministry, Jesus returned to his hometown of Nazareth and began to teach in his childhood synagogue. His citation of the passage from Isaiah and his pronouncement that the text was fulfilled served notice that Jesus fully understood himself as a prophet and particularly a prophet with a mission to the poor and outcast.

Those who had known him as a boy began to comment on his sermon: "All spoke well of him and were amazed at the gracious words [or words of grace] that

Man of the Year
Form small groups. Recall a time when you went back home to where you were raised, visited a place after a long absence, or reconnected with old friends. How did it feel? In what ways was it awkward? comforting? Why?

Being Graceful

How comfortable are you with the idea of a Jesus who offends people? who purposefully seems to displease them? Can you recall other times in the Gospels that Jesus did this?

Jesus did not confront or annoy people just "for the fun of it." What was his purpose? How do you reconcile this with Jesus as a grace-filled Son of God?

Read the Serenity Prayer. Pray it together. Why do you think this prayer has become so important, particularly for people in recovery from addiction? What does it mean to you? As you pray it, does anything in particular come to mind that you should accept with serenity or change with courage? If you wish, name this aloud to your group. Ask for group wisdom to help you know the difference.

came from his mouth" (4:22). No doubt hometown pride was at stake here ("Gosh, isn't Jesus all grown up and educated now? I can remember when he was just about this tall"), but the crowd was clearly charmed and pleased.

However, Jesus seemed discontent to be admired by the home crowd. He wanted the congregation to understand the prophecy, so he followed it with two sharp stories from Scripture (1 Kings 17:1-16; 2 Kings 5:1-14). At the heart of the zingers about Elijah and Elisha is the fact that those prophets were sent to minister to Gentiles not to the Israelites. So by telling these stories, Jesus implied that God is less concerned about the good and upright people of the synagogue than about those whom synagogue members despised and depreciated. Jesus, in effect, told them off for religious snobbery.

Imagine Jesus as a young idealistic seminary student who is invited back to preach to the proud church he attended as a child. There sit his old Sunday school teachers, the retired pastor who wrote him a letter of recommendation, and the members of the choir and congregation who prayed for him. Instead of thanking them, he fixes his eyes on them and accuses them of being a bunch of lost fools. No wonder their complimentary attitude suddenly shifts to a murderous rage!

But such is the energy of Jesus' commitment to the poor and his conviction that God is outraged at the social and economic oppression. Throughout his ministry, Jesus seemed to give little regard to pleasing others. Better to be full of grace toward others than to be graceful, he might say.

Grace: Being Loved, Loving God

GRACE FAVORS

Grace can also mean "favor," "goodwill," or "gift." Banks and businesses will sometimes give you a grace period—extra days (of goodwill) after a bill is due before they levy a finance charge. If you ever happen to meet a duke, duchess, or archbishop, you can address them properly as "Your Grace," remembering that the courtesy title draws from this second meaning of the word *grace*.

Grace as favor or gift is the meaning that will be most important for us as we continue our study, because at root when we think about Grace with a capital "G" is that we are concerned about being in the "good graces" of God.

This is what it means when we remark about an unlucky person, "There but for the grace [favor] of God go I." And this is what *grace* means in the prayer now used by Alcoholics Anonymous but that first appeared in a sermon by theologian Reinhold Niebuhr in 1943: "God, give us grace [favor us with the ability] to accept with serenity the things that cannot be changed, courage to change the things which should be changed and the wisdom to distinguish the one from the other."

MOST FAVORED ONE

Read Luke 2:39-52.

Jesus the prodigy taught wisdom well beyond his years and amazed his parents and listeners much the way he would later do in the Nazareth synagogue. But note how Luke brackets this story before and after with the comment that Jesus was growing in wisdom and in divine favor (the word used

Grace Favors
What are the ways in which you have been in the good graces of someone else or of some group or institution? Have you ever "fallen from grace" or out of favor? What happened?

Most Favored One
Read Luke 2:39-52. What evidence can you find that Jesus was treated with grace? that he showed grace? that he was in the grace of God? What is the difference between human and divine favor? Is it possible for us to lose divine favor? Explain your response.

Study the story of Jesus in the Temple. Because children traveled with women, Joseph could have supposed Jesus was with Mary. Since Jesus was thirteen, Mary would have thought he was with the men. Notice his response in verse 49, indicating a sense of destiny and purpose. How is this sense of purpose tied to God's grace?

Saying Grace
Look up each of the Bible passages and enough of the surrounding passages to establish the context. How is Luke or Paul using "thanks" in these passages? Do you ever express thanks for the same things or in similar circumstances? Do you have a sense that God somehow has responsibility in the good things that happen to you and thus should or could be thanked?

here is *charis* or *grace*). Note also how Jesus grows in human favor (2:52)—a favor he will ultimately lose. first in Nazareth and finally on the cross.

SAYING GRACE

The word *grace* can also mean "thanks" or "thanksgiving." This definition can be found at least a dozen times in the New Testament where the Greek word *charis* is usually translated as "thanks." Look, for example, at Luke 17:9: Romans 6:17: 2 Corinthians 2:14; or 1 Timothy 1:12: "I am grateful [literally, "I have thanks"] to Christ Jesus our Lord. who has strengthened me."

The idea that *grace* can mean "thanks" will not sound strange to those who normally say "grace" at meals. Actually it used to be that one would say "graces" before or after the meal. and often both. This phrase came from the idea that all good gifts come from God. Food is one of God's many "graces" to us. and so it is natural for us to give thanks. or say grace, in return.

One famous prayer at table was penned by the poet Robert Burns (1759–1796):

Do you say grace over your meals? Before or after you eat? Why or why not? Are there some situations (at restaurants, for example) where you are less likely to say a prayer? Why or why not?

Some hae meat and canna eat.
And some would eat that want it;
But we hae meat. and we can eat,
Sae let the Lord be thankit.

Giving thanks at table is fundamental to the Christian life. for it is precisely the giving of thanks that marks a meal among Christians as a communal meal.

Write out a brief prayer or statement of thanksgiving to God that would be appropriate for mealtime, at the beginning of the day or at the close of the day.

FOR ALL WE ARE ABOUT TO RECEIVE

Read Luke 22:14-20.

We are looking at Luke because we may as well stick with a good thing this session. But just as easily we could have read Matthew 26:20-30; Mark 14:17-26; or 1 Corinthians 11:23-26; for these are all parallel accounts of the institution of the Lord's Supper. Note in all these accounts how Jesus gave thanks for the bread and cup before he distributed them. The word for this is *euchariste* (*eu*=well; *chariste*=to give thanks). At its center is our word *charis*: "grace" or "thanks." This is precisely why some churches call their communion service the Eucharist. It simply means "thanksgiving."

The basic fourfold practice of taking food, giving thanks for it, breaking it, and giving it out is found throughout the New Testament. The frequency of its inclusion in the New Testament writings testifies to how central the practice of the common meal was to early Christians. Jesus modeled the practice in John 6:11 when he gave thanks over the loaves and fishes in feeding the 5,000. Paul gave thanks before distributing food on a ship on the morning of the fourteenth day of a dreadful storm at sea (Acts 27:35).

The church still gives thanks over its food whenever it follows the example of Jesus and shares the bread and cup in thanksgiving and memory. What pastors essentially do while they are standing at a Communion table is saying an extended grace over a meal to be held in Jesus' name.

BIBLE

For What We Receive
Compare the four different accounts of the institution of the Lord's Supper (Luke 22:14-20; Matthew 26:20-30; Mark 14:17-26; 1 Corinthians 11:23-26). What differences do you notice among them? Hint: Count the number of cups Jesus uses and how many times he gives thanks. How does the practice of Communion in your church express the basic idea of thanksgiving?

Have copies of your hymnal on hand. Turn in the Communion liturgy to the prayers of thanksgiving and say them together. Or look up the Communion hymns and sing one or two of them. How do they help you understand the gracious gift Jesus has given all humankind and the depth of thanksgiving that such a gift inspires?

FUSING THE WORD WITH MY WORLD

We have concentrated on three of the uses of the word *grace* so far. In fact, we have only scratched the surface. There are many more nuanced ways that the Greek word *charis* is used that we have not yet discussed. Through the course of this study we will meet most of them.

What we have learned is that the Bible pays little mind to the idea of grace as charm, and when it does (as when people at first found Jesus charming), it turns this notion upside down. Judging only by the way this simple word is used in the Bible, it seems that to live a genuinely grace-full life will not be easy or popular. It may mean falling out of the good graces of some people as you fall into the good graces of God. One piece of good news: There are countless meals with Jesus along the way to sustain you.

DISCUSS

Summarize the various ways *grace* has been used in the Bible and the ways you typically think of it. What new insights have come up for you?

CLOSE

If you opened your session today with silent gestures, remind one another of the gestures you used. Think again about the meanings of *grace* that you encountered in this session ("charm," "favor," "thanks").

Discuss: What meaning did each of the gestures express? Did some meanings predominate? Did some meanings discussed in this session not get expressed?

GOD'S RISKY BUSINESS

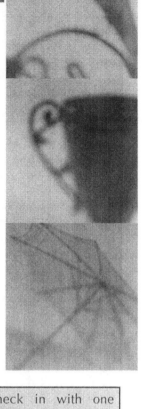

> This session is designed to examine the image of grace in the Old Testament.

In our first session we looked at the concept of grace from a dictionary's point of view, illustrating it with examples from the New Testament. The sense of grace as charm especially was in the cultural air at the time. The use of grace in the religious sense was also common within the Jewish religion well before Christianity emerged. To get a proper sense of what grace means for Christians, it is vital for us to look at some bedrock understandings of God's character that come out of the Old Testament.

To begin, think about the meaning of trust. What is the relationship between trusting others and entrusting yourself to others? Can one claim to trust another person yet continue to withhold large segments of one's identity or life? Or is trust a fundamentally risky and fragile thing that by necessity comes slowly, if at all?

START Check in with one another. Bring newcomers up to date by reviewing the three different meanings of *grace* you discovered in the New Testament.

CASE STUDY Read about Max and Cal on page 28, or use an experience of your own about trust. What makes long-term trusting relationships especially difficult in our time? What are the possible benefits of an attitude of wariness toward others? What are the potential costs? What experiences might make it difficult to trust others or wise not to?

Under what circumstances would you reveal each of these secrets to others? How many of these things might you share with a church group? with your family? In your opinion, what is the relationship between self-disclosure and depth of relationship?

• Details about your medical health • Something about your sexual self • How much you earn • Your age • Your weight • Your personal religious practices (praying, for example) • Trouble in your family history • How much debt you carry • A hidden tattoo • Your Internet history files • Entanglements with the law • Your grades or SAT score • Your social security number • How much you paid for a house or a car

TRUST

Maxine

Maxine is a successful web designer and has a good group of friends, but she often feels lonely. Her parents divorced when she was young, and her mother worked two jobs to make ends meet. Like her mother, Max has learned to be strong and independent. She has had a few loving relationships in the past but feels diffident about making a life-long commitment. Rattling around in the back of Max's mind is the bitter advice of her mother: "You can't depend on anyone but yourself." She understands that this is not advice she can live by for the long years to come, but she also knows that learning to trust others does not come easy for her.

Cal

Cal is bisexual but not "out." He works as a service tech in a car dealership and comes from a relatively conservative hometown and family. Although he is comfortable with his sexual identity, he has good reason to believe that should it become common knowledge he would be reviled at work and home and possibly discriminated against. After several years of friendship, Cal came out to a coworker who asked him about his personal life. Now, although Cal was explicit that his friend should keep his secret, he regrets sharing this dangerous knowledge and vows not to be so careless in the future.

GOD'S DISCLOSURE

Read Exodus 33:12-23.

While Moses was up on Mount Sinai receiving the Ten Commandments, the people of Israel were making themselves a golden calf to worship (Exodus 32). In spite of his intense anger, Moses interceded to God on Israel's behalf. Apparently he was successful, for after some wavering (33:1-3), the Lord promised to stay with Israel: "My presence will go with you" (verse 14).

Then Moses made an outlandish request, especially given the timing: Moses wanted to be permitted to see God's "glory" (verse 18). Astonishingly, the Lord consented at least to some of Moses' request. God hid Moses in the cleft of a rock that would allow Moses to see God's back (literally, God's "after") but not the divine face: " 'I will make all my goodness pass before you, and will proclaim before you the name, "The LORD": and I will be gracious to whom I will be gracious, and will show mercy on whom I will show mercy. But,' he said, 'you cannot see my face; for no one shall see me and live' " (verses 19-20). God does reveal but not all.

The writer of this story is struggling mightily to put into words a holy mystery, using the extreme anthropomorphisms of God's face, back, and hands to try to describe what Moses experienced. As strained as it is, the language beautifully manages to express a clear tension between God's remarkable self-giving and the protection of God's nearness and otherness—God's *immanence* and *transcendence*, to use the language of theology.

It is especially remarkable that God chose to make this self-revelation to Moses at a time when the relationship to Israel was precarious.

BIBLE Compare Exodus 33:12-23 to 24:9-11 when a large group go up the mountain and "see" God. Yet even here the description of what they saw is so unclear that all that is reported is a confused description of the place under God's feet.

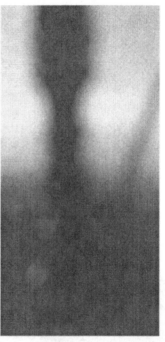

BIBLE Compare Exodus 33:12-23 to Paul's comments in 1 Corinthians 13:9-12 where he concludes, "For now we see in a mirror, dimly, but then we will see face to face." God is both revealed and hidden, and yet the promise is that this veil will someday be stripped away.

God's Autobiography
Read Exodus 34:1-8.
What happened? How
are God and Moses characterized? If you had been in Moses'
place, how might you have felt?

GOD'S AUTOBIOGRAPHY

Continue by reading Exodus 34:1-8.

The Lord initiated the process for renewing the covenant with Israel by having Moses make a new set of stone tablets. (Moses smashed the others when he saw the golden calf.) Interestingly, the first tablets were made directly by God (Exodus 24:12; 31:18). The next morning, in a revelation that seems to surpass what Moses received before (although the details are sketchy here), God came out of a cloud and stood next to Moses, passing before him, proclaiming the holy name (YHWH, an unpronounceable four letters, which is translated in English as *Lord*). The next few verses (34:6-7) are presented as if they are the very words of God, God's own self-description. This remarkable passage includes three central words, each of them providing a deep insight into God's nature. Let's look at the passage more closely.

The passage begins with two proclamations of the holy name: "YHWH, YHWH (The LORD, the LORD)" then continues with a description of this Lord:

Biblical Studies 101: What Should We Call the Old Testament?

Some Christians are beginning to wonder if it is right to describe the first three quarters of the Bible as the "Old" Testament, because that may sound as if it is somehow less important to Christians than the writings in the New Testament. The authors of the writings that make up the New Testament did not think of themselves as writing "Scripture."

In fact, Jesus, Paul, the apostles, and most of the characters in the New Testament were Jewish and would have understood Scripture to mean the Hebrew texts of the Torah, Prophets, and Writings (although the exact Jewish canon, a list of books considered holy, was not formalized until well after Jesus lived.) These writings contain insights into God's character and work in history that we lose if we only read the New Testament: *hesed* is an example. Here are some alternative names that are being used these days: Hebrew Scriptures, the Hebrew Bible, the Inherited Testament, or the First Testament.

Grace: Being Loved, Loving God

- "a God *rahûm*," an adjective that means "merciful" or "compassionate." This word is related to the Hebrew word for "womb" (*rehem*), showing that at the core of God's self-description is the image of God as soft and warm.
- "and *hen*" from *hannûn*, an adjective meaning "the gracious favor that one bestows on another." The noun form *hen*, meaning "grace or favor," occurs 67 times in the Hebrew Scriptures. It is often associated with "face" or "eyes," as in "Noah found favor in the sight [eyes] of the LORD" (Genesis 6:8). When the Hebrew text was translated into the Greek form around 200 B.C., (an historically important version of the Bible called the Septuagint), the Greek word used to translate *hen* was *charis*.
- "a God abounding in *hesed*," a noun meaning "steadfast love," indicating God's intense and unrelenting loyalty, especially to those who are in covenant with YHWH.

Practice your close reading skills. Copy out the two verses of Exodus 34:6-7 on a chalkboard or piece of poster paper. Go over these words line by line. Which image do you find the most assured? the most confused? the most engaged or confrontational? How do these images help you understand the grace of God?

This third word, *hesed*, is especially important and can be found throughout the Hebrew Scriptures. What we learn from this text is that God's commitment to Israel is so sure and deep that no matter how badly they violated God's trust, God remained faithful. Earlier we observed that it appeared that God was wavering in commitment to Israel (Exodus 33:3). Now it appears that the effect of Moses' intercession was to draw out a more fundamental reality of what it means to be in relationship with Israel's God. God keeps divine promises.

The central confession about God in Exodus 34:6-7 is repeated throughout the Old Testament in Numbers 14:18-19; 2 Chronicles 30:9; Nehemiah 9:17; Psalms 103:8; 111:4; 112:4; 116:5; 145:8-9; Joel 2:13; Jonah 4:2; and Nahum 1:3. Look up these passages and compare them to Exodus 34:6-7. Given how often this phrase appears in Scripture, many scholars believe that it is an ancient liturgical formula used in the Temple.

Would you depend on God for • money matters? • help at work or school? • protection for you and your family from crime, accident, or natural disaster? • guidance for a hard decision? • healing from life-threatening illness?

If so, what would such dependence actually look like in real life? What are our responsibilities in these matters? What are God's?

The Basis of Grace

"Protest Theology," following the Holocaust, essentially goes like this: If God is really characterized by *hesed* as the Hebrew Bible insists, then how can one reconcile this with the immense suffering of Auschwitz, or the gulag, or Hiroshima? For many contemporary people, confidence in God's trustworthiness (or even existence) is no longer warranted after these horrors.

THE BASIS OF GRACE

This fierce loyalty of God to the covenant is, in fact, the entire basis of our relationship with God. Think for a minute how it would be if this were not so. What type of a relationship would we have with a God who was more like us: sometimes not entirely faithful or dependable? What if God were like the gods and goddesses of Greek and Roman myth whose dealings with the world were based on whimsy and petty, heavenly squabbles? What about a god whose wrath had to be appeased by human sacrifice?

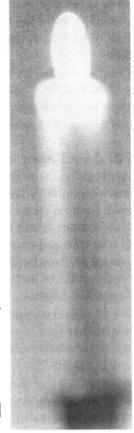

Christians have inherited so much from the faith of Israel but none as important as this insight into God's *hesed* (God's covenant loyalty), the ancient Hebrew way of expressing God's grace, favor, or goodwill to humanity.

As a landless people existing in the harsh conditions of the desert, they came to know a God who would never let them go. They learned to sing "your love [*hesed*] is better than life (Psalm 63:3).

AVOIDING MORE GOLDEN CALVES

In all, this two-verse passage (Exodus 34:6-7) contains seven affirmations of God's grace and commitment to humanity. Notice what this passage does not say about God. It does not describe God in terms of absolutes: perfection, omnipotence, omniscience, eternity, infinity; rather, God is always spoken of in relational terms. They were a people who were struggling with mere survival. Coming out of slavery and wandering in the desert for so long without a home, the central theological concern of Israel was not to describe or understand God philosophically, but to know whether God loved them and was committed to them.

This issue of relationship, however, cut both ways. God's radical relationship to Israel meant that Israel could also offend and anger God. The passage ends with two clear and rather harsh statements, too. God does not ignore those who sin but allows the effects of transgression to echo through the generations.

The Old Testament theologian Walter Brueggemann has observed that the God revealed to Israel is one of complexity, even oddness. On the one hand, God forgives iniquity; yet on the other hand, God remembers it and punishes it. The God described here is not about lambs and bunnies and soft-focus sentimentality—Israel is dealing with a real God who is complex, even dangerous. In Brueggemann's words, God's "reality is marked by an open-ended, unresolved two-sidedness. This God is at the same time capable of inordinate generosity (mercy, graciousness, steadfast love, faithfulness) and an assaulting severity (visiting iniquities). For many people, such an unre-

LOOK CLOSER

Avoid Golden Calves
Study Exodus 34:7 closely. Compare it with Deuteronomy 24:16; Jeremiah 31:29-34; and Ezekiel 18:1-4. Do you bear the blame for the sins committed by your father and mother? by your ancestors? Today, those who were victims or descendants of victims of terrible crimes in the past are often seeking apologies and reparations for their suffering: African Americans whose ancestors were enslaved; Native Americans whose lands were stolen and civilizations dismantled; the "Comfort women" forced into prostitution by the Japanese army during World War II. Does this passage about the character of God apply to these cases? Why or why not?

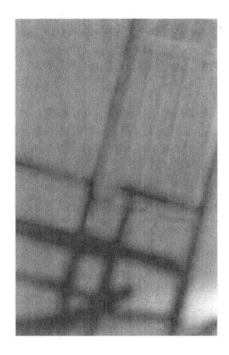

solved quality in God is deeply distressing (*The New Interpreter's Bible*, Vol. I: Abingdon, 1994, page 951).

Brueggemann suggests that we should not try to harmonize these two sides of God or hold that the God revealed in Jesus in the New Testament has grown beyond this dichotomy. Either easy solution reduces the reality and otherness of God and remakes God in our own image. If in our mental image of God, God always punishes wrong-doers, or if God always forgives and forgets the most heinous of blasphemies and crimes, then we are not worshiping a living God but a formula for making ourselves feel better. We are reenacting the story of Israel who made an idol of the golden calf and turned away from the living God.

FUSING THE WORD WITH MY WORLD

The God discussed in this passage is a God seen through the lens of the golden calf incident. It is a God whose mercy and grace extends, not to a people who demonstrated their worthiness to be a partner in covenant with God, but a people who had become profoundly sinful. God extended and firmly maintained a covenant with a group of people who were, frankly, not a very good risk.

Much of the biblical story over both the Old and New Testaments is a record of God continuing to engage in risky behavior: disclosing the divine self to humanity despite a sorry record of broken trust. That is the nature of God's grace. An objective person might ask why being a person of faith sometimes seems to us to be so hard when it is God who takes the bigger risk.

THE NECESSITY OF GRACE

> This session is designed to explore a basic understanding of the relationship between sin and grace.

NEIGHBORS

It was a Polish town called Jedwabne. The German soldiers who had come to town on a summer day in 1941 only had to give permission, a little helpful advice, and stand back and watch while the Polish (Christian) half of the population murdered the Jewish half. Professor Jan Gross of New York University, who tells the story in his book *Neighbors* (Princeton University Press, 2001), describes the way people flocked from all around the countryside to participate in the killing spree—adults were tortured and their children stabbed with pitchforks and burned alive. Of the 1,600 Jewish residents of the town, only a dozen survived.

How can one explain the sudden eruption of absolute evil? Dr. Gross concluded that they did it because they were given permission—nothing would stop them. The ugly implication is that if we knew there would be no consequences, we might kill our neighbors, too.

START

Check in with each other. Open with a prayer of thanksgiving and share concerns for the situation of humanity in the present world.

CASE STUDY

Neighbors
Using a chalkboard or a piece of poster paper, make a list of all the feelings that you experienced in reading this true story, or in hearing similar accounts of mass murder. Be careful to distinguish between feelings and thoughts or opinions about what happened.

Cause and Response
Read the three differ-
ent theories presented
in this section. Do you think people in general are good, bad, or in-
between? Why? Are they born that
way or do they grow that way?

Think together: Why might God
have made human beings the way
they are? How much of our moral
selves is just given at birth and
how much is a reflection of our
own choices? How does your
thinking about the basic nature of
people make a difference to your
politics? to the way you live?

DISCUSS

CAUSE AND RESPONSE

Are people basically good or are they
basically evil? How we answer may make
more practical difference than we first
think. If people are intrinsically good,
then violence and evil are mostly
responses to frustration, ignorance,
poverty, shame, or illness. The best social
policy in that case is one that helps people improve by increasing access to good
education, healthcare, decent jobs, food,
housing, and other basic necessities.

But if people are intrinsically rotten,
then they will only be good when there is
a strong social contract that provides
clear incentives like wealth and prestige
and disincentives like punishment and
public shame. Appropriate social policy
in this case would include enforcing
stricter laws, hiring more police, and
building more jails.

Or perhaps evolutionary psychologists
are right when they say that like other
higher primates we are neither inherent-
ly good nor bad. Rather, our brains
evolved so that we are hardwired with
tendencies for altruistic behavior toward
those who are related to us or like us
(those in our "tribe" or gene pool) and
with tendencies for distrust, fear, and
violence toward strangers and those who
are different than us. In this theory,
down deep we just want our kin to sur-
vive and thrive, and we will do to others
what we must to keep it that way. If this
scenario is right, then smart social policy
might include discouraging the social
isolation of particular groups and pro-
moting cross-cultural education.

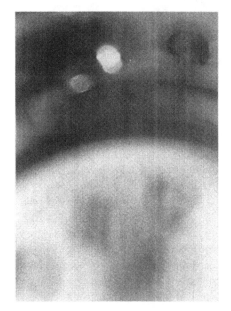

WERE WE BORN BROKEN?

Read Romans 5:12-21.

The Judeo-Christian tradition has always taken seriously the reality of sin and evil even if we have not always agreed on the details. Most people agree that no one is morally perfect, but why is this so?

Tradition says that it all began with the disobedience of Adam and Eve in the garden (Genesis 3). Scholars of the Bible accept this story as a profound religious story that expresses the mystery of the origin of evil in a world created by God. Yet even if this story is taken as history, the question remains: What impact has this disobedience made on future generations? Strikingly, the Old Testament says nothing about original sin (which will be explained shortly), and barely mentions Adam (and never Eve) after the opening chapters of Genesis. (For an exception, see Hosea 6:7.)

Paul argued in the New Testament that humanity is fundamentally broken because of the events in Eden. The actual doctrine of original sin developed later, as we will see, but it was Paul who first provided the rationale. Paul stated that Adam's sin not only brought him death but came to every member of the human family .

Even so, Paul's main concern in this passage of Romans is less to explain the origin of sin than to explain the difference that the death of Christ made (Romans 5:6-9). The righteousness of the "one man" Jesus overcomes the sin and death wrought by the one man Adam.

Were We Born Broken? Romans 5:12-21 is part of a long argument that extends from 5:1 through 8:39 concerning the new life made available through Christ. Form four teams, each reading a different chapter of Romans 5–8.

Read also Genesis 3 to remind yourself of the comparison of Jesus as the second, perfected "Adam" with the Adam of the garden. Make a list or outline of all the ways Christ's life affects Christians.

Back up to include Romans 7:7-13 in your reading of this section. Paul discusses how the experience of the "Law" revived sin in him. What does he mean by *law* here? Using a Bible dictionary or commentary on Romans will be helpful. Outline the argument Paul makes. How exactly does he think that the holy law can be a stimulus for sin?

Read Romans 7:13-25.

But as the newspapers remind us every day, sin and death did not come to a sudden end with the death of Jesus. In essence, Paul's position is that from the standpoint of eternity, sin and death's final power over us was destroyed, and this new reality is working itself out in people by grace. But it seems to be a long and painful process. Paul suddenly shifts to the present tense, indicating an ongoing struggle. He knows what is right, he says, but is unable to make his body do it. It is as if an alien principle has control of what he does (verse 17). Paul's way to resolve the conflict is to throw himself on the mercy of Christ (verse 24).

But this opens another question: Are we in control of our moral lives? Or are we only pawns in a battle of larger forces beyond our control? Can we do good without grace?

DO WE NEED GRACE?

This question was hotly debated in the early years of the fifth century between Augustine, bishop of Hippo (an ancient city in North Africa, not the mammal) and Pelagius, a Welsh layperson.

For Augustine, although some measure of free will remains, we are so tainted by sin that our will is biased toward evil. This is original sin, a disease into which we are all born. It is a power that holds us captive and something for which we bear guilt as members of the human race.

The purpose of God's grace in this line of thinking is not just to help us as we are but to remake us entirely. In the end we will be judged not by what we do but by the action of the free gift of grace. Augustine's theology is hard for many people to swallow because it has led to some harsh conclusions over the centuries (but by no means have these been held by all Christians), such as

- that infants are born sinful.
- that only people who are baptized or who consciously confess Christ are saved.
- that apart from grace we are totally depraved and can do nothing to help our cause with God.
- that God arbitrarily chooses or predestines who will be saved and who is damned.

Pelagius's Turn

Imagine a friend or a colleague asking the questions inherent in Pelagius's argument. Place those questions in a real-life situation and examine how they play out. Or use a situation in your own life when you faced a moral or ethical conflict and then state the consequences. How did you interpret your responsibility for whatever sin was inherent in the situation? for whatever grace? How did God figure in the situation and the outcome?

PELAGIUS'S TURN

For Pelagius, these were all horrible and inescapable conclusions of the doctrine of original sin. Pelagius did not deny that sin was universal, but he insisted that we are born innocent. Even so, all humans choose to sin and for our own sins we are condemned before God. All humans are sinful by their own free choice.

Read Matthew 25:31-46.

This passage seems a challenge to Augustine's view of sin and salvation. Here is a powerful scene of the judgment day in which people are separated according to their deeds in life.

Pelagius would say that Jesus taught right from wrong precisely because God knows that we have free will. To say otherwise is to evade one's own responsibility for sin. Pelagius had a very sober view of his own sinfulness, and he was unwilling to blame an inherited power of original sin for his own wrongdoing.

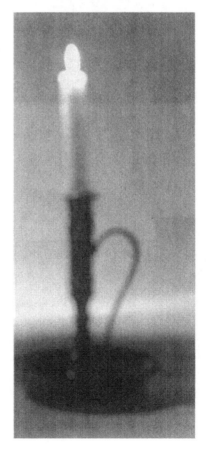

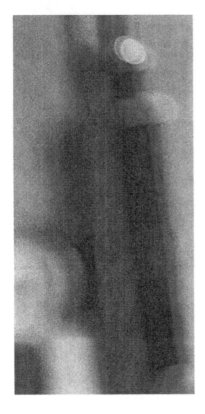

For Pelagius, the purpose of grace is to enlighten us by telling us what our responsibilities are, but it does not assist us to fulfill them. If we cannot do good on our own, he asked, then how can God reasonably hold us responsible for our sins? What kind of a God would punish people for doing something they are compelled to do?

A REJOINDER

Augustine carefully read Pelagius's books, and he noticed the absence of the necessity of God's assistance. If we can be good by the exercise of our free will alone, Augustine asked, then what is grace for? Why should Jesus Christ come? Why do we need to be saved at all? What was the purpose of the cross? As Augustine said of Pelagius, "it is by no means clear . . . what grace he means, or to what extent he supposes our nature to be assisted by it" (*A Companion to the Study of St. Augustine*, Roy Battenhouse, editor; Oxford University Press, 1955; page 219).

In the end, Augustine's view prevailed, and his basic understanding of sin and grace have marked the church ever since, even if every sub-point was not always accepted. Pelagius was declared a heretic by the church and sent into exile.

ORIGINAL GRACE

In the thirteenth century, Thomas Aquinas reprised the question about the necessity of grace in his *Summa Theologica*. He covered all the bases: Can we know anything, do or wish any good, love God above all things, keep the commandments, earn

BIBLE Read Genesis 1–2 and examine God's creativity and purpose. What is the single greatest description of what God created? If this is inherent in all of creation, including people, how would you explain the presence of sin? How does the idea of "original blessing" compare with "original sin"?

Grace: Being Loved, Loving God

eternal life, prepare to receive grace, leave sin behind, or avoid sin in the future without grace?

To these he answered no. No, we cannot do or know anything apart from God's grace, he said, and for two reasons. First, everything there is has been created by God. Nothing exists apart from God's graceful desire to bring it into being, meaning that living outside or beyond the realm of God's grace is impossible. Second, Aquinas believed that human reason is by its very nature constructed to seek out the truth; but all truth ultimately comes from God. So the very way that the human mind functions to make sense of the world is a gift of a God who wishes to be known. Every impulse we have toward the good is always already grace filled.

"Creation Spirituality" theologians like Matthew Fox have argued that churches in the Western hemisphere became unduly fixated on the doctrine of original sin after Augustine. According to this theology, Western churches usually have missed what Christians in the East have characteristically celebrated: that the first tale the Bible has to tell is not about sin but about how God made the world, its creatures, and human beings, and called them very good. Before original sin is original blessing—a blessing that our sins, no matter how horrifying, cannot entirely undo.

DISCUSS

Examine Thomas Aquinas's questions to which he would answer no. Do you agree or disagree with him? Why? Do you agree or not that we (you) cannot know or do anything apart from God's grace? Why? If this is so, what does that mean in terms of all the little bits of daily life and God's role in even the most minute things we think and do?

LOOK CLOSER

Find out more about Matthew Fox and Creation Spirituality by reading one of his books, such as *Original Blessing*, or *Creation Spirituality*. Search the internet for more information. One common criticism of this movement is that it does not take sin seriously enough. After doing some investigation of your own, do you think this criticism is fair or not?

DISCUSS

Living With Ourselves
Consider the case of the killing in Jedwabne or of one closer to home. Think about the persons involved—those who had some measure of control and those who had none or little. What roles did free will, sin, and grace play in the event or situation? Do you think that the world is gradually improving or getting worse? Why? Has Christianity made a substantial positive impact on the overall goodness of the world? How does it influence the shape of morality where you live?

LIVING
WITH OURSELVES

So how do we make sense of an event
like Jedwabne? The killing of children by
children as at Columbine High School? Is
evil something that can be understood?
Maybe we best begin with lament for the
roll call of horrors people have inflicted
on their neighbors, on themselves,
and on the environment.

The work that grace must do in the
world is formidable. We do not need
to dwell on horrors to know that: we
are well enough aware of the ways we act
like the goats of Jesus' parable told by
Matthew. Though Christians have disagreed over Scripture, they have agreed
on this: God's grace flows under us like a
strong river and bears us toward a future
beyond the reach of evil.

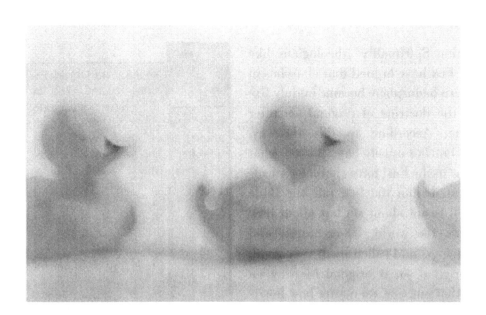

AWAKENING GRACE

> This session will examine one way in which God's grace "goes before" us to lead us into relationship with God.

POCs

Karen Yegoian and Rafik Tonoian, both Jehovah's Witnesses, suffered arrest and jail in Armenia. Their consciences compelled them to refuse to serve in the military, which is compulsory in that nation.

In Brunei, three evangelical Christians—Yunus Murang, Freddie Chong, and Haji Malai Taufick—were arrested under the nation's "Internal Security Act." Their crime? They engaged in activities that authorities believed were aimed at converting Muslims to Christianity. They were denied trial, access to lawyers and family members, and pressured into submitting to religious "reeducation."

In Tunisia, sixteen young people were arrested in July 1999 and sentenced to prison for peacefully protesting student living and studying conditions.

Check in with one another. Begin by asking whether group members have experienced moments of grace in the past week. Times when you sensed an absence of grace? Describe.

POCs

Go to Amnesty International's website (*www.amnestyusa.org*) for more information about prisoners of conscience and "Worldwide Appeals" on behalf of current POCs. Read the cases that A.I. includes from the US. As a group, choose one or more cases and commit them to prayer and write letters on their behalf.

Read Romans 2:12-16. Have you ever thought that what your conscience dictates is what God would have you do or be? When people of good conscience disagree, by what process can we try to determine when this "law" will "accuse or excuse" at the time of judgment?

Those who oppose the government in Tunisia are often subject to detention, even torture.

Amnesty International has named all of these people Prisoners of Conscience (POCs). A central part of A.I.'s mission is to bring such cases to the world's attention and encourage people to pressure governments to clean up their acts.

CONSCIENCE

Conscience
Have you ever engaged in a protest, an act of civil disobedience, or taken other actions because you were driven by conscience? Why? What did you do? Are there other things you do or do not do because of what your conscience dictates? Can you think of an issue for which you would be willing to suffer arrest, torture, or death? What would it be?

Conscience is a powerful force in human behavior, driving people to do things that bring them inconvenience, extra expense, social disapproval, arrest, and occasionally suffering and death. In our nation, people march against racism, boycott companies, refuse medical procedures, write their elected representatives, use cruelty-free products, fight suburban sprawl, oppose tobacco companies, and do countless other things out of their deep convictions that they are obliged to make the world a better place.

Conscience also nags us about more personal things—things we say or do that hurt others, dishonor God, or cheapen our lives. In general, conscience is a process of internal self-evaluation. Psychoanalyst Sigmund Freud theorized that the voice of conscience is evidence that we have internalized the rules given to us by parents and society in childhood. Conscience represses our nonconformist impulses. Contemporary psychologists have seen conscience as the vital way the human self engages in personal moral reflection.

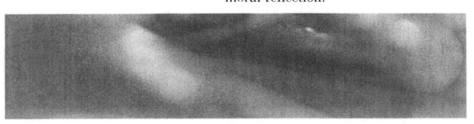

Read Romans 2:12-16.

Paul was influenced by the Hellenistic idea that "conscience" *(syneidesis)* is a universal faculty of the human mind. In this passage, Paul argues that all people have an innate awareness of what God expects of them: "They show that what the law requires is written on their hearts" (13:5). Because we all have this ability, there is no one who can plead ignorance to God's expectations.

Read 1 Corinthians 8:7-13 for a case in which people of good conscience disagreed with one another. The early Christians in Corinth argued whether it was immoral for them to eat food that had been sacrificed to idols and then sold in the market. Some refused, but others thought it was fine. In this passage, Paul repeatedly quotes the arguments of those with "strong consciences" (verses 1, 4, 8).

GOD'S PICK-UP LINES

John Wesley, the founder of Methodism, held that human conscience was a form of God's grace. For Wesley, conscience is not merely a faculty of the human mind, but a chief means by which we are made aware of our sins and led to repentance. This is why he preached "prevenient grace" (from Latin *preveniens*, meaning "going ahead"). Through grace, God prepares us for more grace. Wesley also called it "preventing grace"—grace that keeps us from engaging in evil.

But conscience is just one aspect of prevenient grace. There are many ways that God flirts for humanity's attention and response. For Wesley, a person may be moving through life quite contentedly, "when God comes upon [you] unawares, perhaps by an awakening sermon or conversation, perhaps by some awful providence; or it may be an immediate stroke of [God's] convincing Spirit, without any outward means at all" (from the sermon *Means of Grace*).

Wesley wrote that prevenient grace includes "*all* the *convictions* which [God's] Spirit from time to time works in every child." It could be a fragment of a conversation overheard, a scene from a foreign film, a near-death experience, the silence of

God's Pick-Up Lines
Wesley says that God is constantly "drawing" us towards God through prevenient grace. List as many ways that you can think of that this takes place. What has been your experience of God's "overtures" toward you? When or how have you chiefly felt God's advances?

Wesley also believed that these advances by God could be resisted. Do you think it is possible to completely shut out awareness of God in one's life? Why or why not? Does God ever give up on a person? Why or why not?

Awakening Grace

Look up several hymns in your hELOSER think of examples in other Christian music about how God's grace goes before us, such as "Come, Sinners, to the Gospel Feast," "I Sought the Lord," "Tú has Venida a la Orilla," or "Depth of Mercy." Sing or say some of them together, then review the lyrics carefully. What do they say about God's gracious and merciful presence before us? How does experiencing "a little bit of grace" make us want more? What has been your experience of "sheer grace"?

the woods. the random kindness of a stranger. or the unjust suffering of a friend . . . but suddenly a window in our awareness is thrown open. the possibility of a different or more meaningful life shines in.

This is sheer grace. And with a taste of new grace in our mouths we may well want more. For prevenient grace is not some impersonal broadcast of holy radio waves over the earth: it is always an invitation to respond. Grace is something that we grow more strongly attuned to the more we give it our attention.

Frequently. however. we take these experiences for granted or forget them entirely. as Wesley pointed out: "Although it is true the generality of [persons] stifle them as soon as possible. and after a while forget. or at least deny. that ever they had them at all" (from the sermon *The Scripture Way of Salvation*. 1.2).

IN THE BEGINNING

A popular bumper sticker admonishes us to "Practice Random Acts of Kindness and Senseless Beauty." Prevenient grace is not like that. however. God gives graces extravagantly. but it is neither occasional nor without purpose.

As John Wesley knew. grace is more than a gift God gives us occasionally: it is a continual sharing of God's very life with us. Wesley often equated God's grace with God's love and both with the experience of the Holy Spirit. As we learned when we looked at the Old Testament concept of *hesed* (Session 2). there are no divine rules or regulations administered upon us from points far above the human situation—no management of the world from a distance. God enthusiastically immerses into the situation of humanity all the way "up to the elbows" and well beyond.

In the Beginning

"Practice random acts . . ." is a gracious suggestion. If you have been the beneficiary of such a random act of kindness, especially from a stranger, how have you responded or felt? Grateful? suspicious? obligated? eager to return the favor to the giver or someone else? Is it possible to extend grace to a stranger and have it always taken in the way it was meant? It not, should we just abandon the effort in favor of those we know? Why or why not? Brainstorm new "bumper stickers" or alter the original to convey the idea of grace in a new or better way.

Read John 1:1-18.

This rich passage is sometimes referred to as the "Prologue" of John. It sets John's story of Jesus against a cosmic background. As a hymn of creation it rivals the beauty and soaring language of Genesis 1, which we cannot help but overhear as we read. The Word, John writes, was "in the beginning." It is a light that like the light of new creation shines out and overcomes darkness. But while John wants us to hear Genesis, he intends to take us much further. In Genesis, God's word is the principle of creation (God speaks and the universe comes into being), but in John the Word (Greek *logos*) is fully God, yet actually comes to dwell with humanity. The very principle of cosmic creation becomes human flesh: Jesus Christ.

As the source and principle of all creation, John holds that there can be no knowledge apart from the Word, no true light that does not have the Word as its source. It is "the true light, which enlightens everyone" (John 1:9).

In Jewish writings of the time, *Word (logos)* was often used interchangeably with the word for "wisdom" *(sophia)*. Compare John 1:1-18 with Proverbs 8:22-31. Sophia is there described as having a special role in creation (Proverbs 8:30). Find an edition of the Bible that contains the Apocrypha and also look up Sirach (or Ecclesiasticus) 1:1-10; 24:1-7, and Wisdom of Solomon 7:22–8:1; 9:1-2. Compare and contrast the images of *logos* in John and *sophia* (wisdom) in these writings.

GRACE UPON GRACE

We could say more about this passage, but for now we will focus on the last segment, verses 14-18. As we noticed in the first session of our study, the word *grace (charis)* occurs overwhelmingly in the New Testament in the writings of Paul. In Luke's Gospel, it is occasionally used to describe human gracefullness. It never appears in the four Gospels in a theological sense except in these five verses of John.

John tells us that the Word made flesh is full of "grace and truth" (1:14). The holy Law of the Old Testament was given to God

Grace Upon Grace
Tell stories or think of an event in your own life in which there was an overflowing of "grace and truth" or "grace upon grace." Did you always recognize it as such, or did it seem otherwise—a series of wonderful coincidences, for example—at the time? Did it seem as if you were entitled somehow or if you might just have been very lucky? How did you identify the source of this grace or good fortune at the time (or later)? What does (or did) it reveal to you about God and how God regards you and all others?

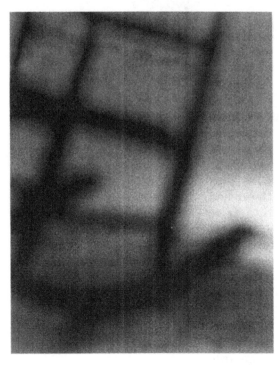

through Moses, but the fullness of God's identity is made known through Christ. It is from this Word that we ourselves receive grace that is overflowing: *charis anti charitos*—"grace upon grace" (1:16).

Grace overflowing. Our whole lives, indeed the whole creation, is infused with grace. We are born into a world saturated with grace. It *preveins* us, it comes before us, a reality far more compelling and important to the universe and its ultimate fate than our sin could ever be. For while sin is something that we impose on the world, grace is woven into its very fabric.

A NEW BEGINNING

Wesley believed that the work of prevenient grace in our lives was felt in three distinct ways.

SMALL GROUP

Break into small groups. Distribute a supply of different kinds and colors of yarn, string, fabric, and scissors. Each group will cut into shape and weave together a pattern that represents for them the way that grace is woven into the fabric of the universe. Is grace a dominant pattern? a slender strand?

- *Pardon*. Prevenient grace cleanses us from the guilt of original sin. Wesley took very seriously the scriptural teaching that Christ's life and death wiped out any universal condemnation of humanity (Romans 5:18).
- *Power*. Although we are not held accountable for any sin but our own, Wesley believed, we are not entirely free from the effect of sin or even its tendency. Prevenient grace, however, partially restores or heals us, at least deeply enough that we can respond to God.
- *Partial Restoration*. Our thorough healing takes time, but prevenient grace restores enough of our understanding so

that we know about God's presence and so that we can distinguish between good and evil. It restores enough of our moral freedom so that we can freely respond to the good we recognize. Prevenient grace restores our will so that we begin to find ourselves yearning for a full measure of God's love. Indeed, this is the whole purpose of prevenient grace. It is an appetizer, a small taste of the full banquet yet to come.

But Only a Beginning
What do all these "firsts" in the John Wesley quote mean to you? Is it possible to be too conscientious? to have too acute a sense of the moral life? Why or why not? How can one know whether a moral inclination is God-given or simply the product of an overactive guilt complex?

BUT ONLY A BEGINNING

In a sermon he preached in 1785, John Wesley gave another synopsis of prevenient grace. It is "the first wish to please God, the first dawn of light concerning [God's] will, and the first slight transient conviction of having sinned against [God]. All these imply some tendency toward life, some degree of salvation, the beginning of a deliverance from a blind, unfeeling heart, quite insensible of God and the things of God" (*On Working Out Your Own Salvation* [II.1]).

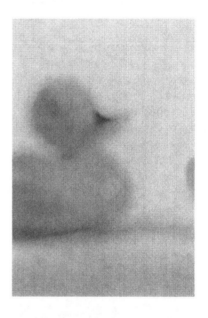

A New Beginning
A dominant metaphor of grace in Wesleyan theology is healing or therapy. Wesley taught that grace actually awakened our dormant "spiritual senses" to things we had previously been unable to experience.

Discuss: How does the experience of God grow or change over the course of human life? Are some spiritual experiences only available to mature people of faith? Are some characteristic only of new converts? Explain your answer.

Saint Ignatius taught the practice of intentionally examining one's conscience as a daily spiritual exercise. He recommended a five-step pattern. Allow at least ten to fifteen minutes for this exercise. A leader may signal the time to move from one step to the next, but do the exercise in silence, and do not attempt group sharing afterwards.

1. Acknowledging. Thank God for blessings or benefits you have received.

2. Asking. Pray for grace to know and correct our faults, as Ignatius noted: "to see myself as I am seen."

3. Admitting. Take each hour of the day in turn; review what you did, note any faults you committed by what thought, word, or deed, you did or chose not to do.

4. Repenting. Ask for God's forgiveness.

5. Resolving. Plan a way to make amendment for any way you injured another person.

Offer the following prayer to close: "God constantly nudges us to awake to a deeper life. May all our senses become newly aware of the signs of grace all around us. Amen."

Notice the emphasis on "first" he gives. Wesley was an astute observer of human life—no matter how compelling and fantastic a new religious awakening may be, life is long and humans are complex. Old habits have a way of returning. The fullness of grace cannot be had all at once.

But following one's conscience is a good place to start. Conscience remains fallible—witness the number of times that people of good conscience disagree—but as an inclination to recognize and respond to what is good, beautiful, and just, Christians can believe that it is a gift of God and a beginning to a deeper life of the Spirit.

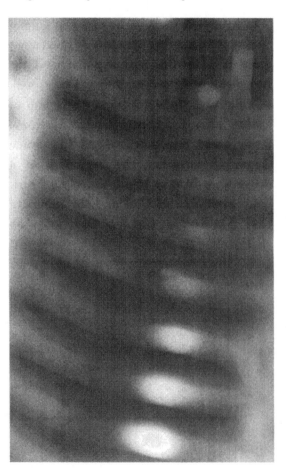

CONVERTING GRACE

> This session explores how grace changes our hearts and lives when we experience conversion of "justification."

A NEW LIFE

It is Sunday morning in the heart of the arts district. Given the liveliness of the streets the night before, a surprising number of the young people who live there are awake and gathering inside a well-worn Romanesque church. As a blues band plays on the stage up front, the diverse crowd grows until extra chairs are needed in the aisles—Latinos, Blacks, Whites, and Asians, gays and straights, women and men. Piercings and tattoos abound. This is no old-line city church kept going by a stalwart group of commuting suburbanites; it is a vital, growing congregation that reflects and ministers to its neighborhood.

The tempo picks up as a huge choir files in. A song leader steps forward with a microcphone to lead a rousing version of the gospel tune "Precious Lord." It is an emotional service. People dance, clap, and cry with equal abandon.

Between the congregational songs, people step forward to sing a solo or tell their stories.

Begin by checking in. Have a brainstorm session. Using a chalkboard or a piece of poster paper, list as many different kinds of emotions that you can in two minutes. Of these, circle those that you would be generally reluctant to express in public. Put squares around those you would be generally reluctant to express in your church. Put an X through what you think one should never express.

Go to Gallup's website, (*www.gallup.com/indicators/indreligion.asp*) to read more about religion in America. Find out more about how religious commitment seems to be related to age. What do the polls say about whether we are becoming a more or less religious nation?

For all their outward diversity, however, those who speak have a strikingly similar story to tell. They were lost in a world of addiction, abuse, prostitution, loneliness, or depression. Then they discovered this remarkable church that taught them about the grace of God. They let go of their fears and turned their lives fully over to God. Since then they have been filled with gratitude, joy, and a powerful hope that has moved them out of the darkness of their former lives into the light of divine love and self-respect. If they choke with emotion as they share their lives, the crowd encourages them with applause and cheers. Someone

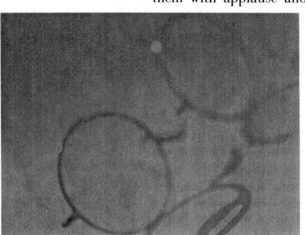

holds a hand or offers a hug. Then the story concludes: They are on the right path now, sustained in their recovery by a community of new friends, and helping others to discover the saving grace of God.

Religion in America
Using a chalkboard or a piece of poster paper, write down a list of the images, feelings, or memories that the following words or terms bring up for you: *camp meeting, revival, born again Christian, evangelical?* How would you label yourself? Why?

RELIGION IN AMERICA

Gallup Organization polls between 1991 and 2001 found that about forty-five percent of people in the United States report that they are "born again" or "evangelical" Christians (*www.gallup.com/poll/indicators/indreligion2.asp*). One would expect that these numbers would imply that our churches are bursting at the seams, but this is not so. Gallup polls found that "the percentage of people with a . . . lived-out faith is far smaller than the overall percentage of religious belief would seem to indicate" (*www.gallup.com/poll/releases/pr010413.asp*)

Since the early 1800s, Americans have lived in a religious culture influenced by revivalism. The frontier camp meeting was, in a sense, an effective religious technology that led people to strong emotional conversions in the short timespan before they had to hitch up their wagons and go back to their farms. For many Protestant churches ever since, the expectation of strong emotional conversions has deeply influenced what we think the purpose of Sunday morning worship services should be.

It is understandable that a fresh experience of God should be an emotional event. Brain scientists have also explained that because of the way the brain is wired, it is very hard to have any life-changing experience unless it is also accompanied by strong emotions. But having powerful emotions and being converted by God's grace are not always the same thing.

SMALL GROUP

In pairs of threes, discuss or debate the statement that "having powerful emotions and being converted by God's grace are not always the same thing." Keep your ideas in mind as you explore justifying grace.

JUSTIFYING GRACE

As we explored in the last session, prevenient grace is theological shorthand for God overcoming the effects of original sin and opening our spiritual awareness. The awareness can move us toward repentance and conversion of life.

In the theology of the apostle Paul, the spiritual movement leads to "justification." It is essentially the full pardon of God for all the sins we have committed. God graciously accepts and forgives us. Like all aspects of grace, this new relationship cannot be earned but only accepted by faith (Ephesians 2:4-10). As Paul wrote in his letter to the Romans: "Therefore, since we are justified by faith, we have peace with God through our Lord Jesus

BIBLE

Justifying Grace
Divide the four Bible references among four small groups. Look up the passages and enough surrounding verses to get the context. How would you describe justification in your own words? What does God do in justification? What do we do?

Christ. through whom we have obtained access to this grace in which we stand" (Romans 5:1-2a).

Paul held that justification. acceptance, or pardon by grace means that a person is ushered into a new life: "So if anyone is in Christ, there is a new creation: everything old has passed away: see. everything has become new!" (2 Corinthians 5:17).

This new lease on life is sometimes called regeneration or the new birth (John 3:5)— hence, being "born again." Like all births. this is just a beginning. It is a new life in God that has to be grown and lived into.

WE WERE WORSE

Read Titus 3:1-8.

The Letter to Titus is the third of what are usually called the "Pastoral Letters" or "Pastoral Epistles." With First and Second Timothy. Titus gives us a good snapshot of the Christian movement as it developed two and three generations after Jesus. The chief purpose of the letter to Titus is to spell out the qualifications for Christian leaders and to guide their teaching ministries.

In this passage. Titus is asked to remind those under his charge to be obedient to political leaders and to seek peace among themselves by showing kindness and courtesy.

In verse 3. we are given the reason for this charge: Because no matter how obnoxious others may seem to you. "we" were the same way and worse. (It is not clear whether this "we" is meant to include all the readers of the letter. all Christian leaders. or only the writer and Titus). But notice how the life before conversion is painted: It is rude. crude. and out of control, as though one was a "slave" to "various passions and pleasures" (verse 3).

The Pauline view of justification shines out in 3:5-8. It is not earned (verse 5) but is a matter of God's mercy. Being justified in God's sight also brings us into the family of those who can hope for eternal life (verse 7). It comes with the expectation that life will be lived differently from now on (verse 8). This passage in Titus expects strong commitment; it gives no indication that strong emotion should be taken as a measure of true conversion.

Read Titus 3:1-8. Is it common among Christians you know for them to discuss their preconversion life in such stark ways? Look at the list of characteristics in verse 3. What would the opposite of each of these be and what would it mean practically for a grace-full life?

WHAT IS CONVERSION?

Justification by faith is a central image of Christian conversion. Conversion is experienced in different ways. Sociologists of religion have studied religious conversion extensively and have found that although it can take many forms, there are three basic types.

- When conversion is *sudden* it is often characterized by emotional crisis and release. Paul himself was apparently an example of this type (Acts 9:1-31).

Baptismal water is described here as an agent of "rebirth and renewal in the Holy Spirit" (3:5). Is your church's practice of baptism as closely linked with the experience of conversion as it is described here? Why or why not? If not, what changes might you propose to how baptism is practiced so that it might become more clearly a sign of washing for rebirth and renewal?

Converting Grace

SMALL GROUP

What Is Conversion?
Break into small groups of three or four. Read this section about conversion and one by one, share conversion stories. Do you find that one of these models (sudden, gradual, socialization) best describes what you went through? Explain how. How do your stories differ? How are they similar? Report these findings back to the large group. How, if at all, are certain types of conversion more authentic than others?

Review answers again to these last questions after looking up the Scriptures in the next exercise.

Study these examples of different types of conversion in Scripture. For Paul's dramatic and sudden conversion story look at Acts 9:1-19 in which the zealous persecutor becomes a zealous Christian missionary.

Look at Nicodemus's gradual experience. As a Jewish leader of the Pharisees, he would look before leaping to any new form of religion. He has a long, rather heady conversation with Jesus in John 3:1-21. By 7:45-52, he is a defender of Jesus among his peers; and by 19:39, he is visiting Jesus' tomb with other disciples.

For conversion as socialization in a Christian family, see 2 Timothy 1:3-7 (also Acts 16:1-5; 2 Timothy 3:14-15).

- When conversion is *gradual* it is often a matter of the intellect—a person is gradually persuaded by the merits of a given faith (John 3:1-21; 7:45-52; 19:39).
- The most common form of conversion is *socialization*. That is, one grows up to accept the faith that he or she was taught as a child or was immersed in by one's culture (Acts 16:1-5; 2 Timothy 1:3-7; 3:14-15).

Conversion can also involve changes in how you are involved in religious institutions. It can be a matter of:

- changing religious traditions entirely (for example, Buddhism to Christianity).
- changing denominations (for instance, from Baptist to United Methodist).
- changing from being non-religious to becoming active in religion.
- changing from being nominally involved to being fully active.

Conversion can (and should) affect one's life at all levels: your intellect, morality, emotional life, and your religious feelings. For those who follow Jesus, however, the only measure of true conversion is our love of God and others (Matthew 22:37-39).

GREAT LOVE

The reformer Martin Luther spoke about grace as God's "forgiving love." Those who suddenly realize that they are wholly and utterly loved by God may experience a rush of amazed gratitude that leads them to do some unusual things.

Read Luke 7:36-50.
This is a moving story of a woman who expresses her conversion with a dramatic and emotion-filled act of love. It is also a

story, perhaps, of the beginning of another conversion, that of Simon the Pharisee.

It is important not to judge Simon too harshly. He had an obvious interest in knowing more about Jesus and had generously invited him into his home to learn more about him. But then this woman unexpectedly entered his home (which in itself was not a breach of hospitality). In addition to being uninvited, she began to act in a way that would be embarrassing for any host. That Simon only grumbled to himself (verse 39) and did not throw her out immediately shows a good deal of restraint on his part.

As a conventionally religious man (a Pharisee), Simon naturally equated godliness with proper behavior, so he was at a loss to know how a supposed prophet would either not know the lifestyle of this woman or seemingly not care. But Simon was willing to listen to Jesus (verse 40). When Jesus told the parable of the debtors, Simon interpreted it correctly (verse 43).

Jesus compared Simon's careful hospitality with this spontaneous act of devotion. Clearly, the woman had done something extravagant and risky. It is a remarkably intimate and unusual act to bathe someone's feet with one's hair. Yet it is this embarrassing intrusion of a woman in a room full of men that Jesus used as the epitome of forgiveness and love. Those who are forgiven little love little. Like so many other places in the Gospels, Jesus implies that it is the recovering sinner rather than the perennially well-behaved who earns God's favor and know the most about true love.

There are twelve characters named Simon who appear in the New Testament. This story, however, is the beginning and end of what we know about Simon the Pharisee. It is inter-

DISCUSS

Think about the gender issues in this story. Have the men ask the women: How do you feel about the idea of a woman bathing Jesus' feet with her hair in a room full of men? Why? Have the women ask the men: Is this intimate way of showing love to someone comfortable or uncomfortable to you? Why?

LOOK CLOSER

In John, Jesus' visit takes place six days before the Passover, also in Bethany, but at the home of Lazarus rather than Simon. It is Mary the sister of Martha who anoints Jesus' feet with her hair and Judas is given the full blame for complaining about the cost of the ointment.

The name *Christ* means "anointed one," an important messianic title. Significantly, Mark, Matthew, and John each have the anointing taking place shortly before Jesus is betrayed and crucified. In Luke's version, however, the anointing is not connected with Jesus' death but his teaching and healing ministries. Instead of a lesson about wasted oil, it becomes a lesson about the nature of true love.

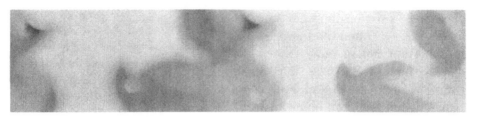

esting to speculate whether this Simon ever really was converted to the life of generous love modeled for him by an invited guest.

WHAT REALLY COUNTS

Robert Capon has written that. "Grace only works on those it finds dead enough to raise" (*Parables of Grace*. Wm. B. Eerdmans Publishing Co.. 1988: page 149). It is the recognition of our own unique dead spots that make them potential subjects for conversion by grace. It is important not to confuse strong emotion with genuine conversion. nor to expect that all persons will be "born again" in the same way. Justifying grace will be experienced in as many different ways as there are different things for which we stand in need of forgiveness.

Justification may be sudden and dramatic, gradual and intellectual. or long-term growth into the faith of our childhood. What makes justifying grace true is not our experience of it but the promise of God on which it rests. What makes it real is how extravagantly we love in return.

Using any version of the Gospel account, write or tell your own ending as a conversion story. Imagine what happened to the woman, the disciples, the host. What of your own experience do you see? How does this story help you understand how God works in our lives to call us into a grace-filled relationship?

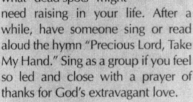

Take some time in silence to reflect on what "dead spots" might need raising in your life. After a while, have someone sing or read aloud the hymn "Precious Lord, Take My Hand." Sing as a group if you feel so led and close with a prayer of thanks for God's extravagant love.

What Really Counts

Have you ever had strong religious emotions? If so, have they been rare? common? What prompts them? What do they mean to you? Are they becoming more common or less in your spiritual life? Why?

PERFECTING GRACE

> This session examines the next steps in grace:
> how to grow in perfect love.

MORE AND MORE

"Grace be with you."

It was common for early Christians to greet one another with the wish that they might be filled with grace. The letters collected in the New Testament almost always begin and end with this blessing of grace. For example, the two letters attributed to Peter both contain this phrase in their second verses: "May grace and peace be yours in abundance" (1 Peter 1:2; 2 Peter 1:2). "In abundance" in the original Greek might be better translated as "more and more" or "in full measure." Later, 2 Peter 3:18 encourages Christians to "grow in the grace and knowledge of our Lord and Savior Jesus Christ."

These verses are curious in that they seem to be asking Christians to increase the amount of grace in their lives. But if grace is always a gift from God and not something we earn, how can we fairly be expected to "grow" in grace? If such growth does happen, how do we know? Does this growth ever taper off or end?

Check in with one another. Begin by praying together a traditional but powerful prayer sometimes called the "Collect for Purity": "Almighty God, to whom all hearts are open and all desires known, and from whom no secrets are hid: Cleanse the thoughts of our hearts, by the inspiration of your Holy Spirit, that we may perfectly love you, and worthily magnify your holy name; through Christ Jesus our Lord. Amen."

LIFE BEYOND THE LAW

Read Matthew 5:43-48.

These verses conclude an important section of what is called Jesus' Sermon on the Mount (Matthew 5:1–7:29). In this part of the sermon, Jesus is speaking about God's expectations for us in regards to the Old Testament Law. Jesus paints a picture of an exacting lifestyle. Not the smallest portion of the law is dismissible (5:18). We are to follow it and teach it without fail (verses 19-20).

Yet even this does not fully describe where our duty ends according to Jesus. In six different ways (starting with verse 21), Jesus quotes the common understanding of the requirements of the Law but rejects it for a much stricter interpretation. The laws against murder and adultery, for example, also imply prohibitions of actively harboring dark or improper thoughts against others (verses 21-30).

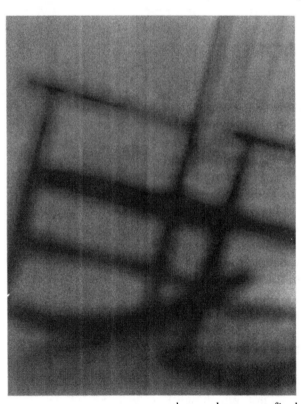

In the same way, sometimes the Law was read as if it only required that we love those to whom we are related or whom we find agreeable (Leviticus 19:17-18). But Jesus counters that we must love even our enemies. Interestingly, the Old Testament never explicitly commands us to "hate your enemy," as Jesus implies (5:43; also Psalm 139:21-22).

Given the brutal Roman occupation of Palestine and the persecution of the early church, this new commandment of Jesus to love enemies would never have been understood in an abstract way. Jesus is not asking us to fool ourselves. People do abuse, undermine, attack, and murder others—they act as enemies. It would be cruel, for example, ever to counsel a victim of rape or abuse to look at their attacker as something other than an enemy. It is immature, on the other hand, to think of people who simply annoy us as our enemies, or to daydream about how everyone should just get along.

Recognizing the political and social reality of his country and of ours, Jesus enjoins us to love our enemies—not in a starry-eyed, forgetful, or emotional way—but specifically and concretely by praying for them and "greeting" or "saluting" them, which in those days would have included the sense of wishing them well (compare with Luke 10:5). To be so well disposed toward enemies is surely not something that comes about naturally or easily. Living life beyond the law must surely require relying on grace.

BE PERFECT?

Loving enemies is a hard enough lesson to swallow. But what can Jesus possibly mean by what follows: "Be perfect, therefore, as your heavenly Father is perfect"? (Matthew 5:48). Surely God's perfection is unattainable by human beings who are limited in knowledge, power, and ability, not to mention troubled by sin.

SMALL GROUP

Divide the six requirements of the law among three or more small groups and examine their meaning. What do you think is the intent of the new interpretation of the law? What might be a current equivalent or example of each one? What does this say to you about your personal duty before God and our duties as a community in Christ?

DISCUSS

Scan through the letters of the New Testament and look at the beginnings and endings of each letter. When you come across greetings and conclusions that contain wishes for grace, read them aloud, giving the citation afterwards.

Discuss: From reading these greetings and salutations, what other experiences of God seem to be used as blessings? How do you normally begin and end letters and e-mails to others? What would it feel like to receive letters or e-mails that wish grace for you? What effect could be obtained if Christians resumed the practice of greeting one another with words of grace?

DISCUSS Does your group have any enemies in common? Do you consider any national or ethnic groups as enemies? If so, why? What active dangers do they pose to you? What would it mean to love them? Do you think you are considered to be an enemy by anyone? If so, by whom and why?

Be Perfect?
Compare Matthew 5:43-48 with Luke 6:32-36, and especially compare Matthew 5:48 to Luke 6:36. How is the call for mercy different from and similar to the call to be perfect as described in this section? from the examples of perfectionism?

DISCUSS **Perfect in Love** Review the section in Session 2 about God's *hesed*. Have you ever experienced this kind of love from another person? observed it in another person? What was it like? Have you ever extended this kind of love to others? When? What kinds of inner motivations may look or feel like love but not be love? Give an example.

So what might it mean to be perfect? Perfectionism takes many forms. Some hear the call to be perfect to mean they should be mistake-free or finicky, as if making the right table centerpieces, getting the car detailed, writing errorless memos, or having a full head of hair is the key to their acceptance. Still others hear it to mean to be highly educated and professionally accomplished. Others might think that perfection means to be free of doubts, fears, or temptations—all those inclinations that pop into our heads or haunt our dreams.

But the call to perfection from Jesus means none of this. Greek philosophy had a concept of moral perfection, but that is certainly not what is meant here in the Jewish world of Matthew's Gospel. The word for "perfect" here is *teleioi*, which means something like "fully mature," "whole," or "in totality." *Teleioi* was used in the Greek version of the Old Testament and in the Dead Sea Scrolls sometimes to signify that one was "undivided" or "without defect" in devotion to God.

PERFECT IN LOVE

Because it comes in the context of Matthew's teaching on love (5:43), it is clear that the perfection that Jesus asks us for is perfection in love. To be perfect as God is perfect is to demonstrate the same kind of love that God showers on us: It is steadfast, undivided, and without lack or defect. This linking of perfection with love is common in the New Testament.

- "Perfect love casts out fear" (1 John 4:18).
- "But when the perfect comes, the imperfect will pass away." Paul here is speaking about how love never ends (1 Corinthians 13:10; Revised Standard Version).

It is not God's abilities, knowledge, power, or even God's moral perfection that we are called to emulate, but God's fundamental character of grace—*hesed*, as we talked about in Session 2.

SANCTIFYING GRACE

Christian thought has often made a distinction between the grace we receive that justifies us and the subsequent grace that we receive to purify us. As we discussed in the previous session, the graceful act of God's justification of us usually leads to the experience of regeneration or the new birth. But this is just a beginning of the life of grace. Like everything in this world that is alive, our spiritual lives either grow or they die. But living things may sometimes continue to live by growing just a little, not reaching full stature or maturity.

God's purpose in all the many dimensions of grace we have studied is never simply to save our skins. It is to fully restore the *imago dei*, the image of God, in which we are all made. Because of the complexity of human life and the depth of sin, this restoration normally occurs in a long process of growth in love and holiness traditionally called "sanctification." John Wesley, and many of his followers since, taught that it is even possible to experience "full sanctification" or perfection in love even in this lifetime. After all, they reason, Jesus would never have taught us to love perfectly as God loves were this not possible for human beings.

Sanctifying Grace
Do you think it is possible to become perfect in love in this lifetime? Why or why not? What would such a life look like in today's world? Does it seem to you common for people to feel spiritually stuck at the level of their conversions? Have you ever felt spiritually stuck? What got you unstuck?

Think about your favorite songs (pop music, ballads, hymns, any musical genre) that have love as the theme. Sing a few, if you wish, or say them together to review the words. Imagine that the singer is you or someone you know. How does the attitude or expression of love fit your experience? Is it mature and well-grounded? pure fantasy? bittersweet? only physical or emotional? How close does it come to perfect love in the theological sense? How do you think about *hesed* in relation to your most intimate love?

⋔OVING ON

The New Testament indicates that growth in grace was deeply important to the early Christians. Upon becoming a believer in Christ. joining the church. and amendment of life. what next? How easy it was. apparently. to stay rooted in the thin soil of a conversion experience. and not to explore God more deeply! But at several places. the New Testament scolds those who do not move beyond their initial awareness of grace.

- In 1 Corinthians 3:1-4. Paul admonishes that he was only able to give the Corinthians spiritual milk because they were not grown up enough. (See 1 Corinthians 14:20.)
- In 1 Corinthians 13:11-12. Paul notes that when he was a child he spoke as one. too. but then he grew out of it.
- Hebrews 5:11-14 observes of its readers that by this time in their journeys of faith many of them who ought to be teachers are still wallowing in the first things they ever learned. They are "drinking milk" rather than digesting "solid food."
- Hebrews 6:1-8 prods Christians to grow: "Therefore let us go on toward perfection. leaving behind the basic teaching about Christ. and not laying again the foundation" (verse 1).

The New Testament is remarkably wise in its understanding of human life: Nothing healthy stays the same. or at least it shouldn't. The expectation is that who we are. what we believe. what we do. and how we experience grace will develop and change. sometimes radically. But that which is centered on love can never be outgrown.

THE MORE EXCELLENT WAY

In John Wesley's own maturity, just a few years before his death, he preached a sermon he called "The More Excellent Way" (1787). In it he wondered whether in his lifetime of ministry he had not encountered two different orders of Christians.

The first order, by far the majority, are those who have experienced God's forgiving grace and have been basically good people in response. They have prayed, worshiped, abstained from evil, and performed a good amount of charitable work in their time. They incur no blame for their lives.

The second order, a smaller number, are those who "used all diligence to attain the whole mind that was in Christ, and labored to walk in every point as their beloved Master." It is easy to preach in generalities. What makes Wesley's sermon so interesting is that he tried to name precisely some of the characteristics of people who live "the more excellent way":

- They go to sleep earlier and wake up earlier to be more healthy and productive.
- They do not let prayer become a mere routine, but devote themselves to a course of rigorous self-examination and lively praise.
- They choose life work and do it always with an eye for honoring God.
- They only eat "plain, cheap, wholesome food," and never too much of it.
- They keep their conversation productive and purposeful.
- They abstain from entertainments that they cannot engage in with a clear conscience.
- They save as much money as they can, use only what they absolutely need to live on, and give the rest away.

More Excellent Way

Do you find Wesley's description of these two different lives compelling or discouraging? something else? Why? Are you surprised at the list he generated to describe the more excellent way? If so, why?

Using a chalkboard or a piece of poster paper, rewrite the list for the group. What would characterize a contemporary life that is completely devoted to living out the life of Jesus? Be concrete. Include in your list something about the use of money, media, lifestyle choices, work, relationships, religious practice. Are there differences of opinion? In what topics? Is it possible for two people to love God and neighbor with their whole hearts and yet still disagree about such things? Give an example. What, finally, do you think is the "more excellent way" for you and for the faith community of which you are a part? Why?

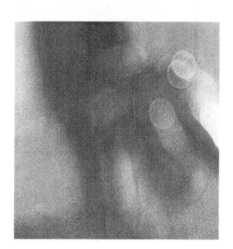

Further Up and Further In

Think of a way that you have sought excellence in your life, perhaps in the world of sports, studies, or work. What did this pursuit require of you? After the discussion in this session, how do you understand grace in terms of growth? Is there something about the nature of grace that now makes you want to pursue it "further up and further in"? What kind of faithful support will help you do this?

Pray again, one line at a time and aloud, the Collect for Purity with which you began this session. Allow time between each line to say aloud, if you wish, what each line may mean to you.

End with this famous benediction from 2 Corinthians 13:13: "The grace of the Lord Jesus Christ, the love of God, and the communion of the Holy Spirit be with all of you."

FURTHER UP AND FURTHER IN

In *The Last Battle*, the final book of his series about the land of Narnia, C. S. Lewis gives a compelling description of heaven. After the final war destroys the old Narnia, the main characters find themselves in a new Narnia. They are tirelessly running ever westward as Aslan, the great lion, urges them to move "further up and further in."

Lewis here invoked a powerful image first used by Paul. Paul compared the spiritual quest for perfection in love to an athlete running to win a race. "Not that I have already obtained this or have already been made perfect," Paul writes, "but this one thing I do: forgetting what lies ahead. I press on toward the goal for the prize of the heavenly call of God in Christ Jesus" (Philippians 3:12-14).

The prize of the life of grace is the very heart of God.

Session 7

GIFTS OF GRACE

> This session will examine how God's grace is at the heart of the gifts we have and are called to use to build the community.

BAD GIFTS, GOOD GIFTS

When the well-known behavioral scientist Robert Sapolsky arrived in Kenya to begin what would be a life-long adventure studying baboons, he was little more than a naive graduate student. He was sitting outside his tent watching hyenas one day when a Land Rover full of park rangers pulled up. Their job, of course, was to enforce the strict Kenyan anti-hunting laws; and the success of his work would largely depend on whether he could gain their trust and support. To his surprise, the rangers flipped open the back of their truck to reveal a dead zebra that they had illegally shot for meat. The head ranger sawed off a hind leg and offered it to Sapolsky, who knew it would be unwise to refuse their gift. They drove off leaving the soon-to-be-ex-vegetarian Sapolsky wondering how one best prepares fresh zebra (From *A Primate's Memoir*, Scribner: 2001; pages 29-31).

START

Begin by checking in with one another. Since this is the last session of this study, take some time to think about things that you have learned together about grace. What questions about grace remain, if any?

DISCUSS

Bad Gifts, Good Gifts
What is your family's practice concerning gifts at birthdays? Christmases? How has gift exchange become simpler or more complicated in your family in recent years? What guidelines do you use at school or work for gift exchange?

What was the best gift you ever received? the worst? What makes a gift appropriate or inappropriate?

Giving and receiving gifts is an integral part of human relationships; but gifts can be appropriate or inappropriate. Poor gifts are known by the negative experience they produce: They induce a feeling of guilt or obligation, they draw too much attention to the giver, or they bring embarrassment or shame.

Good gifts that honor the recipient and are given freely without inducing obligation

Gifts for the Church

Read 1 Peter 4:10-11. Have you ever thought about having a part in the corporate gifts of the church (not just the local church, but the church eternal)? What does it mean to you to know that you do? What does it suggest to you about identifying and using those gifts? Some persons claim to have no special gifts, but the Bible says you do; there is no room for debate about that. If you have the gift for speaking, what does it mean, and mean to you, to think that these words should be spoken as "the very words of God"?

showing that attention has been paid to who the recipient is. Good gifts increase a person's sense of worth and self. They generate positive experiences.

GIFTS FOR THE CHURCH

Read 1 Peter 4:10-11.

Among the controversies that have plagued Christianity, one of the most unnecessary has been about the *charismata*: the spiritual gifts celebrated and practiced by a portion of the church sometimes called "charismatic." Being familiar by now with the Greek word for "grace," *charis*, you may have noticed immediately how it also appears in *charismata*, from which it is drawn. *Charismata* simply means "a gift freely given." In the New Testament, this word is often used to describe special graces or gifts that God bestows on the church for its well-being and growth.

In this brief passage from the first letter of Peter we are given a description of how these gifts should operate in a healthy church. We are to be caretakers of that which we have received. The assumption seems to be that all of us are given different gifts and that the purpose of them is not for personal benefit, but for the benefit of others. A special word is reserved for those who are given the gift or responsibility of speaking. Those who are asked to put into words the faith of the community are obligated to remember that the community will take what they say as "the very words of God" (verse 11).

SMALL GROUP

Break into small groups. Take some time to consider ways that you believe you are gifted. List these on a piece of paper, but do not show it to the other members.

After a few minutes shift the conversation to consider the giftedness of the other people in the small group. Taking one person at a time, let other members of the group describe how they perceive each one's giftedness. Afterward, compare how the group's perceptions compared to self-perceptions. What were the differences?

ΜΑΝΥ ΓΙFTS, ΟΝΕ ΓΟD

Read 1 Corinthians 12:4-11.

In contrast to the description in First Peter, individual giftedness among the Christians in Corinth was apparently divisive and destructive. The Corinthians were interested in the most spectacular and showy gifts. Some entered an emotional altered state of consciousness in which they uttered unintelligible speech. If one could speak in the language "of angels" (1 Corinthians 13:1) or understand spiritual mysteries hidden from others (13:2), it appeared as if one were especially close to God. Competition and individualism was the natural result in such an atmosphere where spirituality was judged by individual ability rather than communal health.

To counter this trend, Paul pointed out to the Corinthians that the many ways in which the church members are gifted all come from the same source: "All these are

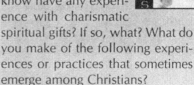

Many Gifts, One God
Do you or anyone you know have any experience with charismatic spiritual gifts? If so, what? What do you make of the following experiences or practices that sometimes emerge among Christians?
• faith healings
• exorcisms
• speaking in tongues
• snake handling
• being "slain in the Spirit"
• channeling the dead
• predicting the future

Compare 1 Corinthians with Romans 12:6-8 and Ephesians 4:11-16. Make three lists of the different gifts mentioned in each passage. Which ones are mentioned frequently? only once? Do any of these gifts describe what you do in your church? in your life's vocation? Are there gifts that you wish you had? Which ones and why? What do you think is your greatest spiritual gift (which may or may not be listed in Paul's writings)? How do you use it? How does Paul use the metaphor of the body in each of these passages?

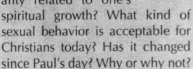

Embodiment
Read 1 Corinthians 7:1-7; 12:12-31. How is sexuality related to one's spiritual growth? What kind of sexual behavior is acceptable for Christians today? Has it changed since Paul's day? Why or why not?

activated by one and the same Spirit" (12:11). It is striking how diverse the gifts listed here and elsewhere by Paul really are. To put it another way, God has no apparent interest in people being the same or doing the same things. Rather, God revels in the vast differences and abilities we all carry into our lives with the church.

Paul's list of spiritual gifts here is interesting (verses 8-10), but notice how unintelligible speech and interpretation, the most highly prized among the Corinthians, comes last in the list! (See also 14:1-5.) Some students of the Bible have read this list of gifts as exhaustive, but it is not. Paul was providing examples of gifts, not a list of the only gifts possible.

EMBODIMENT

Read 1 Corinthians 12:12-31.

Given the information we have in Paul's letters, it seems that the Christians living in Corinth were deeply influenced by the underlying spiritual dualism of Greek culture. In a dualistic worldview, being spiritual is thought to be unrelated to the reality of the body. Paul's preaching against promiscuity sometimes causes modern people to cast him as a sexual spoilsport. At root, however, Paul inherited the Jewish understanding of the deep interrelatedness of the whole human being—body and soul. Rather than suppressing sexuality, he actively encouraged couples to marry and stay sexually active, not depriving one another (1 Corinthians 7:1-7).

Paul also emphasized the importance of the body in his teaching about the afterlife. He taught that at the end of time Christians will experience what Jesus did: a resurrection and transformation of the body, not a disembodied soul flying off to heaven (15:1-55).

Paul even argued that God's grace is most fully known in the imperfections and sufferings of bodily existence, as exemplified in the cross of Christ (2:1-5). Paul found in his own physical hardships that God was speaking to him, saying "My grace is suffient for you, for power is made perfect in weakness" (2 Corinthians 12:9).

LOOK CLOSER

Think about your hope for life after death. How do you envision it? (1 Corinthians 15:1-55).

It is natural then that Paul uses the analogy of the body to understand the nature of spiritual giftedness. Just as there is no spirituality that somehow hovers above or apart from the human body, so there are no spiritual gifts given for the sake of individuals alone. In contrast to the highly individualized tendencies in contemporary pop spirituality, Paul takes for granted that individuals cannot be genuinely spiritual by themselves. This would make us strangely "disembodied"—removed from the community of mutual giftedness that challenges and enriches our lives with God.

DISCUSS

What do you think of Paul's conviction that God's grace is known in physical hardship and weakness (1 Corinthians 12:9)? Can you think of an example? Are there people for whom this might not be perceived as good news? Are there ways that this saying of Paul's could be taught that would be harmful to others? If so, what? How might you reconcile this teaching with Jesus' ministry of healing?

KNIT TOGETHER

Read Ephesians 4:11-16. Paul's metaphor of the body of Christ challenges us to recognize how interdependent we are on one another, even when it comes to grace and salvation. Too often we think of grace in individualistic terms: the traditional pattern of describing grace—prevenient, justifying, and sanctifying—that we have considered together in this book can lend itself to thinking that God is primarily interested in saving individuals. But recall that God's *hesed*, or covenantal faithfulness, was something given to Israel as a whole, a community of faith. So we should not be surprised when this passage from Ephesians explicitly links God's gifts to individuals with the growth of the whole body together: "Until all of us come to the unity of the faith and of the knowledge of the Son of God, to maturity, to the measure of the full stature of Christ" (verse 13).

The idea of the church as a body is a remarkably organic image. The church is not a static entity, nor one that has an ideal form. There was no "golden age" of the church that we can or should try to recreate. Like every living organism, the church must adapt itself to its environment to thrive. It is expected to grow and change through the years. But at the same time, to chase the latest spiritual fad or teaching is a sign of immaturity (verse 14). We are to recall that Christ is the head of our embodied community (verse 15). When we do so, we are knit together tightly and function well. The church is never in danger of losing its true identity as fashions change and the generations roll on.

GRACE FOR LEADERSHIP

Read 1 Timothy 4:11-16.

Many of the texts about spiritual gifts or graces in the New Testament highlight gifts given for leadership in the church, like pastoring or teaching. Here, Timothy is urged not to let his particular gift as a leader go to waste. (See also 2 Timothy 1:6.) The letters to Timothy reflect a later stage of the early church when it was becoming more institutionally complex, and certain configurations of gifts were necessary for community leadership. On the whole, however, the New Testament does not think of some of God's gifts to individuals as better than others. All are for the benefit of the whole and are equally needed.

How do you perceive the work of full-time or ordained leadership in the church? Is it a job that is highly esteemed? Why? Have you ever considered going to seminary? being a pastor? Why or why not? Have you known someone who seems to have suitable gifts for ordained ministry whom you could encourage (1 Timothy 4:11-16)? Are there other forms of church leadership that you practice or have considered? Do you think the shortage of ordained ministers is a problem for the future of the church? a hidden blessing? Why?

Our culture, on the other hand, tends to value only particular types of giftedness: good looks, athleticism, business acumen, and intelligence. It usually expresses its sense of value with big paychecks. Other forms of giftedness are significantly less well rewarded: social work, teaching, and artistry are examples. The ordained ministry is another. One of the realities of the contemporary church is that fewer people are hearing or responding to a call for ordained ministry.

Churches across the globe are already changing the ways they do things because of this change. Responsibilities like worship leadership, preaching, or pastoral care that were once reserved for ordained pastors now often are shared among many people. Is this a return to a more ancient pattern of the church where many gifts are shared for the benefit of all? Is this one more sign of waning church status and influence and of the lack of interest in ordained, full-time ministry?

Find out how the church which you are a part structures its leadership. How are they appointed? What processes of qualification and ordination are required? Invite an ordained leader to your class to speak about his or her
• sense of calling
• perception of the work
• joys and sorrows in the work
• sacrifices made along the way

THE GIFT OF OUR LIVES

Author and theologian Frederick Buechner has written that "a person's vocation is where their deep joy meets the world's deep need." Is this not a bit idealistic? In choosing our life's work, we sometimes find ourselves torn between what we love to do, or are gifted to do, with having to make a living. There are other times that we are gifted to do more than one thing but that the limits of our time and energy require us to choose. Sometimes hard choices have to be made.

It may help to remember that in a true community of faith we do not have to do it all. Paul's advice to the Corinthians about spiritual gifts actually did not begin with advice at all, but with a word of appreciation that they all have received the grace of God and have been extraordinarily gifted by God, not lacking in anything they need (1 Corinthians 1:4-7).

The image of the church as the body of Christ is a powerful challenge to our individualism and self-reliance. Our individual vocations are simply one part of the larger vocation of humanity to respond to God's manifold grace. Our lives with God and with one another are to be one continuous exchange of gifts.

CASE STUDIES

Getting Started

Use any of these cases in place of or in addition to the cases in the sessions as a means of stimulating discussion.

Case 1: Sam and Tad

Sam is a divorced mother of two. Among her neighbors in the apartment complex is Tad, whom she sees now and again as they come and go. Recently, he has knocked on the door a couple of times with what seemed to her as flimsy excuses: to borrow laundry detergent or remind her that there would be construction on the street the following morning. She senses that he is interested in her. Sam has not felt uncomfortable around Tad in any way; in fact, she might be interested in him under different circumstances. But keeping a job and raising two kids is enough for her for now.

Recently, Sam noticed Tad's mail piling up, and she learned he has been hospitalized with a dangerous infection in the lining of his heart. She learned from another neighbor that he would be discharged soon and face recovery alone in his apartment. Sam wants to be neighborly but feels as if to offer help to Tad might give him mixed signals. Part of her does not care if it does.

- How do you prioritize between the biblical duty to love your neighbor and the duty to care for one's immediate family?
- Where does Sam's own longings for relationship fit into this equation?
- Where would you identify God's grace in this story?
- What are Tad's opportunities for expressing grace?

Case 2: Brian

Brian, twenty-three, describes himself as a "born again" Christian. He has a part-time, low-level job in the city working for a record company. He is finishing a degree in arts administration (with a music emphasis) and aims for a job in the growing Christian music industry. His job mainly involves handing out swag (free t-shirts and other items given out as marketing tools), hanging posters, and talking with music store owners and fans about new groups on the scene. Occasionally he is asked to hand out freebies for a group or rap star that uses violent, sexist, or blasphemous language. He does not feel comfortable doing this but believes that overall he can make a difference within the industry. He also values the contacts and experience he gets for the work he plans to do someday in Christian music. There are no Christian music companies in the city where he lives where he might seek employment.

- What are Brian's alternatives?
- How could each of these alternatives express his faith commitments?
- Where might grace work in this story in ways Brian may not see yet?
- What do you think about the rising Christian music industry? Must Christians limit themselves to Christian alternatives to popular music, movies, books, and entertainment?
- As a person of faith, have you ever had to compromise your ethics in the work you do? Under what circumstances? What are the possible effects of such compromise on the person of faith?
- What would a life that required no compromises look like?

Case 3: Brita and Gil

Five years into their marriage, Brita and Gil are confronted with the reality that they are unable to have a baby. They look ahead to consider two alternative futures for themselves. They could begin the process of adoption, but given the long waiting lists, they know that their best chance for an adoption is for a child who is older, has special needs, is of a different ethnic background, or from abroad. As admiring of other couples as they are who do this, they are not convinced that they are ready to take on such enormous responsibilities and challenges.

The other alternative is for them to pour themselves into their careers, do charity work, and be good aunts and uncles to their nieces and nephews. As Christians they are seeking to know what God's will for them might be, what the purpose of their life together may be, and how best to share the love they have with others.

- Does Christian marriage necessarily include procreation?
- Should Brita and Gil have been trying for a baby of their own if they are not willing to adopt?
- Do the qualities of a grace-filled marriage require the presence of children?
- What steps or procedures might you be willing to go through if you wanted children but were unable to have them naturally?
- In what ways do you see grace evident in Brita and Gil's situation?

Case 4: Han Sil Kim

The Rev. Han Sil Kim is the female pastor of a Korean-American congregation outside of Atlanta. The congregation has been thriving as an increasing number of Korean families have settled in the local neighborhood. The congregation gathers on Sunday morning for worship and Wednesdays for Bible study and *Tong Song Kido* (a form of prayer in which all the people pray aloud at the same time).

In the past several weeks, however, one of the most active church members, Min Chun Seo, has been talking a lot about the baptism in the Holy Spirit. He prays in tongues and has been sharing with the others about this rich experience, suggesting that their spiritual lives are not complete without it. A few other members have been influenced by this and by visits they have made to a local charismatic church. Pastor Han is not herself a charismatic but knows that Korean churches are deeply divided over these issues. She has begun to hear complaints that the theology and practices of Seo are causing divisions in the congregation.

- Under what circumstances is it all right for a congregation to split?
- Why are such divisions common between non-charismatic and charismatic Christians?
- What things can both sides learn from each other?
- What might Pastor Han do in this situation to help?
- Having studied the nature of grace, what kind of ideal outcome would you imagine here?
- What are some of the particular challenges that an immigrant community and church may face? What responsibilities do established churches have toward communites with challenges unique to their situation?

SERVICE LEARNING OPTIONS

Enhance your group's understanding of balanced Christian living by implementing some of the service projects mentioned below.

IDEA #1: Learn More About the Holiness Tradition

The doctrine of sanctifying grace has been the cornerstone of what is called the "holiness" tradition in America. One of its most important beginnings was in the "Businessman's Revival" of 1857–58, and the writings of Phoebe Palmer. Find out more about this revival and tradition using books about the history of Christianity or searching on the internet. If your congregation is not one, find a congregation in your area that uses the name "Holiness" or emphasizes this doctrine. Visit this congregation at worship. Invite a leader from that church to come speak to your church about what they understand by holiness, how one finds it, how it is experienced, and whether it is necessary for salvation.

IDEA #2: Reflect Grace

Get your group involved in an ongoing relationship with a local charity: a shelter for abused women and children, a city or county jail, a food pantry, or a nursing home, for example. The ongoing relationship is what is important here. Avoid doing one-time, pop-in acts of ministry when volunteers abound (especially at Christmas or other holidays). Instead, make a commitment to be in one setting and let the relationships grow until members of your group get to know individuals who are being served and vice versa. Allow your group plenty of opportunities to debrief. Return to the themes of this study regularly, and talk about how the meanings and experiences of God's grace may change for you.

IDEA #3: Share the News of Grace

Organize and plan a retreat for another group based on the theme of grace using what you have learned in this study. Sponsor a group of persons that would normally not be able to go on such a retreat or spend time in a natural setting: working mothers, retirees, foster children, bereaved women and men and youth in single parent homes. Pray for attendees and group leaders ahead of time. Plan the retreat so that it will become for them an experience of God's grace: cook excellent food, prepare well for group discussion and study about grace, and allow plenty of free time and time for silence.

IDEA #4: Signs of Grace

Make worship banners for your congregation using themes and Scripture excerpts discussed in this study. Some possibilities for this are Exodus 34:6-7; Psalm 63:4; Matthew 25:35; John 1:14; 2 Corinthians 12:9; 1 Timothy 1:12.

Another option would be to make baptismal banners for children and adults being baptized. The banners could read, "(*Name*), A Child of Grace" or "(*Name*), By Water and the Spirit." Include an appropriate symbol such as a font, dove, or shell.

Instead of banners, create stained-glass windows with themes of grace. This can be cut easily with a jigsaw into a circle or another shape. Divide the shape into sections using lines of black paint. Then have the different members of the group take responsibility to paint a symbol of grace within. This decorative art glass can be a gift to the congregation or a permanent reminder to put in your group's space to remind you of this study.

CPSIA information can be obtained at www.ICGtesting.com
Printed in the USA
LVOW030340191011

251061LV00006B/45/P